THE
ULTIMATE
BOOK OF
SALES
TECHNIQUES

THE ULTIMATE BOOK OF SALES TECHNIQUES

75 WAYS TO MASTER
Cold Calling, Sharpen Your Unique
Selling Proposition, and Close the Sale

STEPHAN SCHIFFMAN
America's #1 Corporate Sales Trainer

AVON, MASSACHUSETTS

Published by
Adams Media, a division of F+W Media, Inc.
57 Littlefield Street, Avon, MA 02322.
U.S.A.
www.adamsmedia.com

ISBN 10: 1-4405-5024-7
ISBN 13: 978-1-4405-5024-9
eISBN 10: 1-4405-5025-5
eISBN 13: 978-1-4405-5025-6

Printed in the United States of America.

10   9   8   7   6

This publication is designed to provide accurate and authoritative information with regard to the subject matter covered. It is sold with the understanding that the publisher is not engaged in rendering legal, accounting, or other professional advice. If legal advice or other expert assistance is required, the services of a competent professional person should be sought.

——From a *Declaration of Principles* jointly adopted by a Committee of the American Bar Association and a Committee of Publishers and Associations

Many of the designations used by manufacturers and sellers to distinguish their product are claimed as trademarks. Where those designations appear in this book and F+W Media was aware of a trademark claim, the designations have been printed with initial capital letters.

This book is available at quantity discounts for bulk purchases. For information, please call 1-800-289-0963.

Contains material adapted and abridged from *The 25 Sales Strategies That Will Boost Your Sales Today*, by Stephan Schiffman, copyright © 1999 by Stephan Schiffman, ISBN 10: 1-58062-116-3, ISBN 13: 978-1-58062-116-8; *The 25 Sales Strategies They Don't Teach at Business School*, by Stephan Schiffman, copyright © 2002 by D.E.I. Management Group, ISBN 10: 1-58062-614-9, ISBN 13: 978-1-58062-614-9; *The 25 Sales Habits of Highly Successful Salespeople*, by Stephan Schiffman, copyright © 2008 by Stephan Schiffman, ISBN 10: 1-59869-757-9, ISBN 13: 978-1-59869-757-5; *The 25 Most Common Sales Mistakes and How to Avoid Them*, by Stephan Schiffman, copyright © 2009 by Stephan Schiffman, ISBN 10: 1-59869-821-4, ISBN 13: 978-1-59869-821-3; *Negotiation Techniques (That Really Work!)*, by Stephan Schiffman, copyright © 2010 by Stephan Schiffman, ISBN 10: 1-59869-827-3, ISBN 13: 978-1-59869-827-5; *Upselling Techniques (That Really Work!)*, by Stephan Schiffman, copyright © 2005 by Stephan Schiffman, ISBN 10: 1-59337-273-6, ISBN 13: 978-1-59337-273-6; *Cold Calling Techniques (That Really Work!)*, by Stephan Schiffman, copyright © 2007 by Stephan Schiffman, ISBN 10: 1-59869-148-1, ISBN 13: 978-1-59869-148-1; *Closing Techniques (That Really Work!)*, by Stephan Schiffman, copyright © 2004 by Stephan Schiffman, ISBN 10: 1-58062-857-5, ISBN 13: 978-1-58062-857-0; *Sales Presentation Techniques (That Really Work!)*, by Stephan Schiffman, copyright © 2007 by Stephan Schiffman, ISBN 10: 1-59869-060-4, 978-1-59869-060-6; *E-Mail Selling Techniques (That Really Work!)*, by Stephan Schiffman, copyright © 2006 by Stephan Schiffman, ISBN 10: 1-59337-744-4, ISBN 13: 978-1-59337-744-1; *Ask Questions, Get Sales*, by Stephan Schiffman, copyright © 2005 by Stephan Schiffman, ISBN 10: 1-59337-112-8, ISBN 13: 978-1-59337-112-8; and *Stephan Schiffman's Telesales*, by Stephan Schiffman, copyright © 2003 by Stephan Schiffman, ISBN 10: 1-58062-813-3, ISBN 13: 978-1-58062-813-6.

Dedication
To Justin Eli Heffernan, his sister, his mother, and his father

Acknowledgments

Special thanks go to the people at Adams and F+W for always being behind the work that I do. I could not really expect anything to happen without Karen Cooper and Peter Archer, who produce magic. Thanks to Monika Verma at Levine Greenberg. To Daniele, Jennifer, Josh, and Toby for their support. My special thanks, appreciation, and love to Anne.

Contents

INTRODUCTION

Your biggest competitor is the status quo.

This book contains my top tips for salespeople, honed and refined over the years. In many ways it's the ultimate product of more than three decades in this business. It's the result of training more than half-a-million salespeople, of going on thousands of sales calls, and of making hundreds of thousands of phone calls.

Yet in this book, I can tell you nothing—*nothing*—that's more important than this: Your biggest competitor is the status quo. *That's* what you have to overcome.

I mean this in two senses. The first, which I've drummed into salespeople for a long time is simple. The prospect to whom you're talking during your sales appointment or your cold call is *happy with what he's got*. He has no defined need. If he did, if he wasn't happy, he'd have called you.

Salespeople are often taught to look for problems, or even create them. That's bunk. For the most part, if a customer has a problem, she or he will resolve it themselves.

Instead of this problem-centric approach, look at things this way: What you're fighting against is whatever way the customer's accustomed to doing things, whatever service he's using, whatever product he's employing. From his point of view, the status quo seems to be working; your job is to help him understand why it isn't. You have to change him from what he's doing (even if it appears to be nothing) to what you want him to do. You have to change him.

I'll talk a great deal about this problem of the status quo and how to overcome it. It's key to creating an effective cold call and a killer sales pitch.

These days, when I'm addressing groups of salespeople a lot of what I talk about focuses on innovation—a key word. Innovation, after all, is what separates you from the rest of the pack. It's what makes the difference between good and great. Ninety-nine percent of us these days are selling a commodity product! What will get you the sale in the face of this is the degree of your creativity. If you look the same as the other salespeople who are trying to sell essentially the same thing as you, you'll get nowhere.

To spark that creativity, you've got to have insight into the customer: what they do, how they do it, when they do it, whom they do it with, and perhaps most importantly, *why* they do it that way. Once you understand that, you can find innovative ways of showing them how you can help them do it better.

People buy because they believe that what you're selling is better than what they currently have. Your challenge is to demonstrate that fact to them. And how can you possibly do that unless you understand what they're doing with the product or service they're currently using? The answer is, you can't. Hence the value of insight.

Keep these words in mind as you read through the chapters that follow: *insight . . . creativity . . . innovation . . . different.*

Today there's a second sense in which the status quo is your competitor.

The business landscape is changing, and it's changing forever. We saw dramatic indications of this when the U.S. economy (and much of the world economy) crashed in 2008. The stock market plunged, sometimes 800 to 1,000 points in a single day. Home prices plummeted as the housing bubble burst. Unemployment soared above 10 percent, and the financial structure of the country teetered on the brink of apocalypse.

Fortunately, we pulled back, and things improved . . . slowly. But even though this was the most dramatic sign that the business landscape had been altered, the signs of fundamental change were there much earlier for anyone who cared to read them. Beginning in the 1980s with the growth of computing power, we entered an age in which communication and information exchange increased exponentially. When I was younger, there were computers at Yale and MIT that took up whole buildings. They were, on the whole, a bit less powerful than the laptop computer with which I'm writing these words.

Changes in information exchange led, almost inexorably, to the development of the World Wide Web and the Internet. Thanks to e-mail, we now had instant communication with remote corners of the globe. Documents, including text and images, could be sent at the speed of light. Information—and misinformation—proliferated. We found ourselves swimming in an alphabet soup of strange acronyms: VoIP, ICANN, TCP/IP, and so on.

Gradually, even the most technologically conservative (among whom I number myself) had to admit that our old way of doing business was gone forever. With this, there came a new realization: for salespeople to be successful in the twenty-first century, we must engage in a process of continual reinvention. It's not enough to say, "Well, I use e-mail instead of sending a letter now, and I keep files on my computer instead of in a filing cabinet." We have to constantly question the whole way in which we sell.

Anything short of that, and you risk being left behind. The speed at which technology and the landscape it influences are changing continues to accelerate. This means it's not enough to change once; you have to *continually change*. You have to reinvent and rethink.

Reinvention means examining what you do, how you do it, when you do it, and why you do it. It's in many ways parallel to the process I outlined above about gaining insight into your customers—only this time you're gaining that insight into yourself. The goals that you had five, ten, or fifteen years ago probably sounded great back then, but how do they sound now? Has the new sales landscape made them outdated or stale? Are you still living in the past decade, trying to sell in ways that belong in a museum? Time doesn't stand still, and neither should you.

Does that mean that I'm advocating throwing away all the techniques I've developed over the years? The ones I've taught to tens of thousands of salespeople? Of course not. This book is a testimony to the timeless nature of many of my sales principles:

- You have to ask questions.
- You have to let the prospect talk.
- The object of the cold call is to get the appointment.
- You have to keep track of your numbers.
- An objection is an opportunity.
- You must know the personality type of the person with whom you're dealing.

All of these things remain true. What's changed is the context in which you apply these techniques. The key to selling today is insight and innovation. You've got to be willing to try different things. If some of them don't work, fine! Who cares? You tried them—that's the main thing. As someone once said, success depends on your ability to fail early and often.

Today, too many salespeople are selling as if it's the 1950s or 1960s. Listening to them, I sometimes feel as if I'm on the set of the television show *Mad Men*. It's like we're in a time warp.

Such salespeople will get sales . . . a degree of persistence and determination will yield some results, no matter how bad the technique. The point is that salespeople who resist change are wearing themselves out—frustrating themselves, their company, and their clients by refusing to see that the world is different.

Customers today are smarter and savvier than before. They have access to a vast array of information—the Internet. Not all of that information will be good, and part of your job now is to help them sort through the confusing amount of nonsense to see the nature of their problem and what they can do about it. I've always said that sales, when it comes down to it, is about helping the client. That's never been more true than today.

In this book, you'll find techniques that will help you do that. These are the basis of strong, sound, honest salesmanship. At their core, they haven't changed for me in the past thirty-plus years.

But remember: Just because the techniques haven't changed, don't think you're wielding them in the same context as before. Stop and look around you. Take stock of the kinds of questions your clients are asking, how you're communicating with them, and how they're communicating with each other. Find out about their changing needs and problems. Ask them the right questions.

And then get ready and sell!

Stephan Schiffman
New York City
May 2012

PART I

MY SALES PHILOSOPHY

My sales philosophy is pretty simple, really. It comes down to just a couple of points:

- As a salesperson, your job is to help the client do things better.
- The only way to do that is by finding out how and why the client is doing things now.
- That means you've got to ask the client questions.
- And listen to the answers.

There are lots of other elements to a good sale, but unless you start from these basics, you'll find that all you're really doing is collecting rejections. On the other hand, once you put the client first and start really *listening* to what she or he is saying, you'll quickly discover that the client can do a lot of your work for you. They're the experts on their business, and they know what the challenges are. What they don't know is how you can help them. That part's up to you.

Sales Technique #1

Know What You Want Before You Walk in the Door

Not long ago, someone sent me a cry for help. He wrote, "My manager says I'm spending too much time researching the company and not enough time working out what should happen next in the relationship. Shouldn't I know something about the company before I go in?"

I'm a little torn here—I don't like to get between a salesperson and his manager. However, I'd say this: Don't over-research—but do spend a little time gathering the relevant facts. Find out the basics about the company. In today's selling environment, there is no excuse for "cluelessness" about the company's products and services. Take a few minutes to pull up the target company's website. Ask yourself: Who are this company's customers? Which of our success stories would be most relevant to this company?

When you've got the answers to these questions, you should probably move out of "research mode" and think about a different kind of preparation for the meeting.

It's just as important to know what kind of next step you plan to ask for at the conclusion of the meeting. In other words, what is the Next Step you want to get to from this meeting? Specifically: What are you planning to ask for at the conclusion of the meeting? Another meeting to review a preliminary proposal? Another meeting to connect with the president of the company? A phone conference at a specific date and time to review technical details? A formal commitment to work together?

Remember, the Next Step must be helpful, logical, and easy for the prospect to agree to. It must also be connected to a specific date and time. And you must ask for it *directly* before you leave the meeting. Be sure you plan a *primary* Next Step—and a *backup* Next Step, just in case the first one doesn't work out.

Sales Technique #2
Prepare Questions Ahead of Time

Here are a number of questions you should consider asking during the all-important information-gathering phase of your meeting.

- "How's business?"
- "What would you have done in such-and-such an area if I hadn't called you?" (Or: "What made you decide to call us?")
- "What are you trying to make happen here over the next thirty days?"
- "I'm just curious—what do you do here?"
- "How does your company sell its product/service?"
- "How many people work here? Do they report to you?"
- "How many people do you work with who operate out of other locations?"
- "How do you maintain a competitive edge in an industry like this?"
- "How is your organization structured? How many offices/locations do you have?"
- "What are you doing now to grow your business?"
- "What are you doing now to reach out to new customers?"
- "What are you doing now to stay close to your existing customers?"
- "What are you doing now to service your accounts better?"
- "What are you doing now to track what your branch offices are doing on a daily basis?"
- "What are you doing to make it easier for customers to respond to your mailings?"
- "What made you decide to make X a priority right now?"
- "What kinds of new customers are you trying to attract?"
- "Who do you consider to be your biggest competitor? Why?"
- "How do you distinguish yourself from companies like X, Y, and Z in an industry like this?"
- "Is your industry changing? How?"
- "What was the last quarter/year like for you?"
- "Why did you decide to work with ABC Company?"

Whatever questions you ask, *review them ahead of time.* We tend to fall back on what is most familiar to us. Be sure that what's most familiar to *you* as you walk in the door to the meeting is the first four or five questions (at least) that you'd like to ask during the course of the meeting.

Know—and practice—the first few questions you plan to ask at the meeting. This is vitally important because you will be in an unfamiliar setting with an unfamiliar person during your initial meeting. That equals stress, and during stressful situations, you will naturally revert to that which is most familiar to you.

Sales Technique #3

Ask Six Types of Questions

Let's look at six basic question groups that can form the basis of an initial sales call:

1. What the prospect does.
2. How the prospect does that.
3. When and where the prospect does what he or she does.
4. Why the prospect does it that way.
5. Who the prospect is currently working with.
6. (Only ask after you've addressed numbers one through five.) Whether and how you can help the client do what he or she does better.

Questions in each of these six groups have a specific objective that will not vary, no matter how you decide to structure the question.

1. What Do You Do?

Even if you believe the prospect is engaged in a business with which you feel you're familiar, at the outset of your relationship you're not familiar with the unique challenges, opportunities, crises, and compromises that this particular prospect faces on a daily basis. You don't yet know about the organization's history, the typical profiles of its target customers, or the level of success or failure it has achieved in reaching and satisfying those customers. Similarly you don't yet know about the career path of a particular contact you've hooked up with, his or her position of influence within the organization, or the specific way his or her job relates to the personal and business goals, formal or informal, that we all strive to achieve on some level.

2. How Do You Do It?

These questions determine the means the organization uses to attain its essential business objectives. They also cast light on what tactics an individual prospect uses to reach personal goals in a business or career context. Even if you believe the prospect is using a system or service that is similar to those of your other customers, and even if you know that the customer is currently buying a certain product to achieve a particular aim, you're not familiar with the specific applications or product uses this customer has implemented or rejected. You don't yet know about the organization's past experiments in finding effective ways to attain important objectives. You don't yet know what benchmarks are in place or being contemplated, nor do you know what product-related or system-related successes and failures the organization has experienced. Similarly, you don't yet know about the methods your contact has found (or rejected) when it comes to attaining success or fulfillment on the job.

3. When and Where Do You Do It?

These questions focus on the time frame and physical location of the target organization's operations. Is the business strongly affected by seasonal patterns, or does it operate year-round at essentially the same level? Is a particular element of the business something the company is just introducing, or has it been a mainstay of the organization's operation for some time? Does the organization operate out of a single location, or are there a number of branch offices or satellite facilities? Is the organization highly centralized, with all the initiatives either coming from or subject to the approval of a headquarters office? Or is the target organization a more autonomous unit of a larger operation? Even if the structure, business patterns, and overall business profile of the target company strongly suggest to you that it is similar in all essential respects to existing customers, you must determine the specifics for this unique organization.

4. Why Do You Do It That Way?

The answers to such questions cast a light on the priorities and decision-making process at that target organization, either on the group or individual level. Even if you believe that their decision-making process is substantially similar to that of other customers of yours, you do not, at the outset of your relationship, know how the person you're dealing with—or the organization he or she represents—makes decisions. You don't yet know about the organization's formal and informal lines of authority, its corporate culture, or the degree to which the target organization embraces a group-oriented or individualistic style of problem resolution or purchasing. Similarly, you don't yet know about the individual contact's predisposition when it comes to making decisions or approving purchases—if, indeed, he or she is authorized to approve purchases at all.

5. Who Are You Doing It With?

These questions will help you determine whether another independent supplier is currently working with your target organization and, if so, which one. Even if you have done extensive library research or personally purchased or used the target organization's product or service, and therefore feel you have a reliable indication as to what vendors the organization is using, you must resolve the issue definitively.

6. How Can We Help You Do It Better?

Warning! This is an advanced questioning category. Don't ask it before you have developed enough information by means of Questions One through Five. Questions in Group Six are meant to elicit the organization's or prospect's input in developing your formal proposal or to help finalize the implementation of that proposal. Yes, you read that right: In the best case, you will not write or otherwise dictate the proposal outlining what you can do for the prospect. Your aim is to allow the target organization to become the source of the information you deliver when it comes time to "make a pitch." You're going to do this because winning specific input to the content of your proposal, often through posing Group Six questions, will win buy-in on the part of the prospect, and it will substantially increase the likelihood that the product or service you deliver will meet the organization's specifications exactly. By the same token, you will use Group Six questions to find out how you can build long-term person-to-person alliances by helping your contact attain the career or performance goals that matter most to him or her.

Sales Technique #4
Be Punctual

Not long ago, a salesperson came in to see me on a sales call. He was fifteen minutes late and didn't understand why I was annoyed at his tardiness. But think about it. Did you ever go to a doctor or dentist who made you wait for twenty-five minutes—after you'd rushed to get to his office on time? There you are taking a taxicab or driving at breakneck speed in order to get to the dentist for your four o'clock appointment—only to have to spend twenty minutes waiting? That's pretty aggravating, isn't it? Why on earth should we subject our prospects to those experiences?

A salesperson needs to be punctual. Period. He needs to respect his own time, as well as the time of the individual that he or she is going to see. When a prospect blocks out time for you, you have to move heaven and earth to make the meeting happen at the time you've committed to—and that usually means planning on making your way into the office five or ten minutes before the appointed time.

Treat your own time and the time of your prospect with respect. You can do this by:

- Scheduling "hard" appointments ("Yes, I'll meet you at ten on Tuesday morning) around nearby "soft" appointments ("I think we can meet at one, but you'll have to call me to confirm the meeting in the morning."). That way, if your "soft" appointment falls through, you haven't made a trip for no reason.
- Use your off time to compose thank-you letters—but don't do this during the day.
- On those rare occasions when you can't make a scheduled meeting as the result of a dire emergency, call ahead and explain the problem—or try to arrange for a manager or colleague to stand in for you.
- Buy yourself a personal scheduling aid—whether written or electronic—and use it each and every day.

- Never overbook yourself. If you can't make a certain date and time, say so up front and try to schedule your appointment for a date that's not as full.
- Remember who's in charge. If your client needs a few extra minutes to resolve an office crisis before sitting down to meet with you, don't stew about it in the waiting room.

Sales Technique #5

Find Out What's Changed

A salesperson sat down opposite me and said, "My work often involves customer service. What kinds of questions should I be asking to improve relationships with my company's clients?"

Some months ago, I wandered into a Brooks Brothers store. My aim was simple: I wanted to buy a pair of suspenders. That was *all* I wanted to buy. The gentleman at the counter stared at me blankly when I stepped up and looked at him. I said, "I'm here to buy some suspenders." He pointed and said, "Over there."

Having received my marching orders, I walked in the direction he had pointed. I picked out a single pair of suspenders. I paid for them. I left the store. That was the end of the exchange.

A week or so later, I went to an electronics store. Once again, my aim was simple: I wanted to buy a basic clock radio. A clock radio was *all* I wanted to buy. I meandered into the store. I stepped over to the counter and looked at the woman by the cash register.

"Hi, there," the woman behind the counter said, smiling.

"Hi," I replied. "Can you show me where to find a $20 clock radio?"

Please bear in mind that that really was *all* I wanted to buy. And yet, at that point in the conversation, something amazing happened. The woman behind the counter said, "Sure. Just out of curiosity, though . . . what brings you to the store today?"

What a great question! She was actually interested in what had recently *changed* in my life. Clearly, *something* had changed enough to make me decide to walk into her store. She wasn't clear on precisely what it was, and she wanted to find out. So she asked.

I answered her question by explaining that I had just moved to an apartment nearby, and that, since the apartment was bare, I had no way of waking up on time in the morning.

She smiled and showed me where the clock radios were. I picked out a model. Then she asked me whether I wanted to look at a television set. Well, that certainly made sense. I was camping out in an empty apartment; I was likely to be in California for a while, which meant I was in the market for a television; I'd already made the trip down to the electronics store. Why not at least take a look at a floor model or two? "Sure," I said. "Why don't you show me where those are and let me take a look at what you have?" There were other questions as well. Did I want to look at CD players? Microwave ovens? Cordless telephones?

An hour after having walked into a store intending *only* to buy a $20 clock radio, I left with $2,000 in merchandise. All because one person had the sense to ask me about what I had *done* that had caused me to change my pattern and walk into her store.

Sales Technique #6
Use Fallbacks

A while back, I found myself in Dallas, Texas, working with a high-tech company. I was looking at notes that detailed people whom the company's sales representatives had called without making a sale. I was going through page after page of notes, and I kept noticing that, for the most part, the space labeled "Comments" read simply "Did not buy." So I started to inquire a little bit further. I tracked down some of the salespeople who had filled out the sheets, and I asked, "Mr. Smith here, we've got him marked down as 'Did not buy.' Why didn't he buy?" For the most part, there was no real reason. All I would hear was, "He wasn't interested." Then I'd ask the rep what the company's focus was—what it did during the course of the average day, how it kept its customers happy and its competitors baffled—and reps often had no idea!

These lists of thousands of "no interest" companies were in fact particularly promising fallback opportunities. I know because I called that list of "no" answers myself, and I closed 10 percent of the people on the list!

Part of the reason the prospects I spoke with were more responsive to me than they had been to the earlier reps was that I did a little bit better job of interviewing than the other people had. (For instance, I asked questions like, "How are you handling such-and-such now?" and "I'm just curious, why didn't you buy from us last time around?") But that wasn't the *whole* reason I was able to sell to that group. The truth is, rejects don't stay rejects forever. Time passes. People leave jobs or get promoted. Competitive challenges shift.

You and I can increase our sales totals by 5 to 10 percent simply by using call fallbacks. When we hear a no from a prospect, it often means only that the prospect has decided not to buy from us right now—not that the prospect has decided not to buy anything, ever, from anyone. For example, if your prospect's company cannot exist without widgets, they're buying those widgets from somebody. If you're a long-distance seller, the prospects you deal with are almost certainly buying long-distance from *somebody;* it just may not be you. So when you hear "No, we're not interested," what that may really mean is, "We're pretty happy with what we've got right now, so we don't feel like talking to you right now." So who's to say things won't have changed four or five weeks after your call?

After a sufficient amount of time, call your "old" prospects back and find out whether the same person you spoke with last time is still in charge of buying what your company sells. If you reach the same contact, say something like the following: "Listen, I understand you didn't buy from us six months ago, but I'm just calling today to find out how things are going in your widget acquisition department, and to see if you have any new projects up and running." And if the contact has changed, you can start over with the new person.

You can get creative when it comes to calling fallback opportunities. I've worked with reps who've gotten great results by saying, "You know, Mr. Jones, we were having a sales meeting and your name came up and I was thinking that you and I haven't talked in a while." Or if they have to leave a message, they'll simply give their number and say, "Please tell Mr. Smith I was just thinking about him and wanted to talk to him for a moment." Try it yourself. You may be surprised at how well fallback prospects react to that simple statement: "I was just thinking about you."

Sales Technique #7

Don't Focus on Negatives

I've worked with many salespeople, and I've come to the conclusion that there are some people who simply spend their whole careers inventing and/or reinforcing obstacles.

Everyone's seen this in action: the water cooler gripe sessions, the behind-the-back gossiping, the snide remarks on off-days. The potential topics are innumerable. Office politics. Perceived defects in the product or service. Impossibly tough competition. Endless personal problems. Unfair commission schedules.

Now, don't get me wrong. We all have problems, every single day. But some people enter the ring half-beaten, and some enter considering the battle half-won. A successful salesperson must fall into the latter category; a persistent negative outlook will not only make it difficult for coworkers and supervisors to work with you—it will make it difficult for prospects to work with you.

It's common for me to hear a salesperson complain, "Steve, you don't understand how much is expected of us here." My feeling is that most of the time this is nothing more than a martyr act on the part of the salesperson. I've met with hundreds upon hundreds of sales managers, and their goals are usually pretty clear-cut: get good results from the staff. Not necessarily walking-on-water results, but at least keeping-your-head-above-water results.

If you're not making sales, complaining about everything in sight is only going to compound your problem. Not only will you be wasting valuable time you could be using to talk to new prospects, but you'll also lose perspective you need to identify and resolve the problems you're having.

Many companies have had the experience of having a salesperson perform poorly in a certain territory, complaining that "the market is saturated" within it. Take that person off the territory, put someone else on it, and—shazam!—sales take off, saturation or no saturation. The difference? Usually, the first salesperson fixates on limitations, while the new rep brings no preconceptions to the work, and sees fresh opportunities as a result.

Selling is difficult work; no one is saying it isn't. But you must be able to isolate problems, deal with them, and then get down to business. Stay positive. Stay upbeat. You are your own greatest asset; focusing on negatives keeps you from performing at your peak.

Sales Technique #8
Show Your Competitive Spirit

In my view, if you are a salesperson, you are a member of an army, and your army is at war. Fortunately, this type of war presents a great advantage over the standard type: nobody dies in it. But that fact doesn't diminish by a single millimeter the importance of a competitively oriented winning spirit; nor does it decrease your need, and your company's need, for sound battlefield strategies and tactics.

Too many salespeople think of themselves as on their own. In fact, your company has made an immense investment in you and will succeed or fail on the battlefield, in large measure, based on your performance and the performance of your coworkers. You share with a number of other people a common goal: success for your firm. To the degree that your company succeeds, you will succeed; to the degree that your company fails, you will fail.

You're not alone. You're on the front lines, fighting for customers, and the fight is a serious one. If you or your company doesn't take it seriously, you'll lose customers to competitors and eventually "die"— i.e., go out of business.

You must be absolutely dedicated to victory in gaining and keeping satisfied customers, because there is almost certainly someone else out there who wants those customers just as badly as you do. That someone will fight for your business, and fight to diminish your success as a salesperson in your company. You must act aggressively to keep this from occurring.

How do you develop a competitive spirit? There are a number of ways.

- Keep an ear open for intelligence about your business rivals. You talk to customers all day long; find out what your competition is doing, and, just as important, what they're saying about you.
- Report problems immediately to superiors. If you learn of a customer problem with your product or service that seems serious

enough to warrant some rethinking, don't keep this to yourself. Tell the "brass" so something can be done immediately.

- Develop a team mentality. Others in your company—administrative people, production people, others in the sales department—are all working toward the same goal you are: success for the firm. Avoid pointless conflicts with coworkers. Share crucial information that will help your company surge ahead.

- Set goals and then go all out to attain them. Consider your daily schedule to be a battle plan, and then give your every effort over to the goals you establish.

It's the companies that have good lines of communication, clearly established goals, and deep commitment to the attainment of results that will flourish in the coming years—and their salespeople will be at the head of the parade.

Sales Technique #9

Take Pride in Your Work

Some years back, during a question-and-answer period, I asked the participants in a training program to call out the reasons their company should be considered number one in its field.

I stood there in front of the flip chart, marker in hand, waiting. No response. After a little while, a hand went up. "Yes?" I asked. "You know, Steve," the man said (and I'm paraphrasing him here), "we may be number one on raxilated widgets, but when it comes to looking at world mid-sized widget production, I think we actually rank around number four."

"No," a woman called out from the back of the room. "No, six. Mid-sized widgets, we just got the new rankings, we're sixth."

Another pause.

"Okay, well that's interesting to know," I said. "Anything else? What is there that really makes this company great? Anyone?"

A man in the front row cleared his throat.

"Yes?"

"The new cafeteria," he said slowly, "is certainly nice."

Just then, a younger fellow asked to be recognized.

"Yes? What is it about this company that really gets you going?"

He looked surprised. "What?" he asked. "Oh, no, I just wanted to say something. Mort mentioned the cafeteria. They've had some plumbing problems, I just thought I'd let everyone know it's out of commission this week."

"Then," said Mort, "I take back what I said about the cafeteria."

You see my point. When asked to list positive aspects of their work environment, the group either put forward petty complaints or said nothing at all.

If you can't stand behind what you do and where you do it with every fiber of your being, why bother? Why show up in the morning? Why do something that, clearly, you do not enjoy doing? Why ask people to buy your product or service if you don't believe in it?

If you don't take pride in your product or service, and in the organization that stands behind it, you will not be successful. If you focus only on the negatives, the obstacles, the reasons you can't sell the way you should—guess what? You won't sell the way you should.

Pinpoint factors that mark you as superior to your competition. Become comfortable discussing those factors in an optimistic way. In short, talk your organization up. Don't just do this at work. Mention where you work and why it's great at parties, social gatherings, conventions—everywhere. (By the way, this will not only build your optimism about the business but also expose you to a whole new universe of potential customers.)

Suppose you have a real problem with your company. Suppose the reason is rooted in some legitimate, deep-seated objection. Like you have a moral problem selling what you sell. Or a supervisor engages in persistent, subtle (or maybe not-so-subtle) sexual harassment.

Does any of that mean you shouldn't be enthusiastic about where you work?

No. It means you should be enthusiastic about where you work, but you should work somewhere else.

Be proud of where you work, and what you do for a living. You'll see that results will soon follow.

Sales Technique #10
Keep Up to Date

Knowledge is power.

Suppose you walked in to see a current customer on an appointment, and your contact had lost an arm since you'd last seen him. Would you notice?

Granted, something that obvious probably wouldn't get past you. However, there are clues and tip-offs that are, from the point of view of the prospect's business, just as blunt—clues that are visible from the moment you walk in the door, but that many salespeople miss.

What is going on in the businesses of your clients? Do you know? If there were a major layoff in the offing, would you hear about it? Is the business doing well? Is a merger in the works? Are key people happy with your product or service, or is it something a budget-cutter might consider expendable?

Too many salespeople tend to think of "closed sales" as static things. But as I stressed in the introduction, these days *nothing* in business is static. The sad truth is, no business exists for the sole purpose of purchasing your product or service. If your customers do well, you will do well—and, conversely, if they do poorly, you will do poorly. Whatever the case, it is to your advantage to have accurate information ahead of time.

Observing the prospect closely, making an effort to understand exactly what's happening at his or her business (and why), will help you gain a broader outlook on the whole environment in which your company operates.

Of course, watching your prospects firsthand isn't the only weapon at your disposal. There are innumerable reports, journals, and newsletters available to you—and if you have many clients in a given industry, it's a good idea to keep up with that industry's trade news.

A salesperson I know named Marcia had been trying to get in touch with someone at a large company with regard to her company's courier service. She was getting nowhere, and when her contact asked her to "send along some information," she was convinced that she'd reached a dead end. Still, she dutifully e-mailed the information, but nothing happened for weeks on end. She wrote the account off.

Six months later, she received a call from her contact at the firm. Could she come in for an appointment right away? She could, and did, and made a big sale. Curiosity got the better of her, though, and at the end of the meeting she asked: why had they waited so long to respond? The answer: the company's main competitor had begun a new program that required courier service. Marcia's clients didn't want to be left behind.

Had Marcia kept up with industry publications and/or gossip, she might well have been able to tell her contact how a courier service was working out for others in the industry—and closed the account months earlier.

Who does your prospect sell to? Who are your prospect's competitors? How do these competitors sell? What are the main differences between the products and prices of your prospect's firm and its competitors? What is the prospect's market share? What is the prospect's perceived market share? How does your prospect plan to deal with new obstacles? New opportunities? Are any new technological breakthroughs on the horizon? How do all these factors affect decisions about whether or not to buy from you?

Avoid needlessly complex and drawn-out research, but keep your eyes and ears open, and read essential publications. The more you know, the better off you'll be.

PART II

PROSPECTING FOR CLIENTS AND EXPANDING YOUR BASE

As I've said in all my books, particularly *Cold Calling Techniques (That Really Work!)*, any salesperson who doesn't spend a lot of time on the phone prospecting for clients is going to be awfully lonely awfully quickly. Expanding your base isn't just something you do as an added bonus; it's the life's blood of your work. Sure, you can keep selling to the same group of clients over and over again. But in the long run, that's a recipe for a shrinking commission. You need to look for opportunities to grow your pool of clients—and be creative about it.

Sales Technique #11

Keep Prospecting at the Front of Your Activity

One of the biggest mistakes that we make is we convince ourselves that we don't have to prospect on a regular basis. Mediocre salespeople have a deep aversion to one simple principle that successful salespeople always find a way to embrace: cold call effectively—every day—no matter what.

I learned the importance of prospecting some years ago when my business got very busy. We got an assignment in August that sidetracked everyone in the organization.

We stopped prospecting for about two months. It was incredible the amount of work that we had to do on that assignment, and every trainer and every staff person was involved. You know the rest of the story, don't you? You guessed it: in October our sales plummeted. It was December before it started to build up again, but, of course, December is a light month, and it wasn't until January that we saw the light at the end of the tunnel. I promised myself that we'd never go through that again.

The key is to keep prospecting on a regular basis. Making the sale is important, but it's not as important as managing your prospects. And the key to that is to replenish your base of prospects with new appointments.

There are four steps to the appointment-making process that takes place during a cold calling (or prospecting) call: the opening, the interview, the presentation, and the appointment. The problem is that most salespeople spend an inordinate amount of time worrying about what they are going to say in the opening. They think that if they can find a nifty grabber of an opening statement, they can forget about the work in the other three steps.

Of course, you do have to begin with a compelling opening statement that sounds (and is) intelligent. It can't sound phony or unrealistic. A good gambit might be about work that you've done successfully for somebody else. So a typical cold call from one of my top salespeople would open with something like the following: "Good morning Mr. Jones. This is Mary

Smith from D.E.I. Sales Training. The reason I'm calling you today is that a couple of months ago, I finished working with the XYZ Company, and I put together a program that increased their sales by 42 percent this quarter over last year. What I'd like to do is stop by next Tuesday at three and simply tell you about the success I've had for them."

By using that kind of statement, you create a meaningful basis for a conversation based not on what you can do for the prospect (about whom you now know little or nothing), but on what you've done for someone else.

What happens next? The prospect is going to respond to you, and that response shouldn't take you by surprise.

The responses that arise out of a statement like the one you just read are usually going to have some connection to what the prospect does. Not what *you* do, but what the *prospect* does: "We don't do sales training." "We handle all that in house." "We don't use trainers we haven't worked with before." "We just have absolutely no interest."

A superior salesperson is going to effectively turn that response around by saying something like this: "You know, Mr. Smith, that's exactly what a lot of my customers said to me before they saw how our programs could complement their existing training programs. What kind of in-house programs are you conducting now?" In other words, you use their response to focus in on one of the questions about what the prospect's company is doing right now.

After you listen carefully and jot down the information you receive, you're going to repeat your request for an appointment.

Prospect every day—and keep an eye on your numbers. Where appropriate, set new targets for yourself. Develop a set of targets that makes sense for your industry and your income goals, and then commit to the front end of your sales cycle by making the calls you need to make, day after day, no matter what.

If you conduct your prospecting calls in the way I've laid them out above, and you do it consistently—devoting perhaps an hour every day to the process—then you'll get the appointments you need. No doubt about it. And just as important, you should be able to avoid the peaks and valleys.

Sales Technique #12

New Leads Mean New Opportunities

It's a dream come true.

You're on the job, minding your own business, when suddenly someone calls, seemingly out of the blue, and virtually asks you for business. Wow!

I know what the first temptation is. You want to close the sale. Life is tough enough; you spend all day building, establishing, persuading. Now along comes The Sale You Deserve, and you're sure as heck not going to let it slip through your fingers. So you start to move in.

Don't.

It will take some discipline. (Let's be honest; it will take a lot of discipline.) But if you really want to move the lead from the other end of the receiver onto your commission check, I promise you that the surest way to do it is to take a deep breath, count to three, and follow three simple steps.

1. Back off and establish some kind of relationship. Exchange a few pleasantries and get a feeling for the kind of person you're talking to.
2. Find out what's going on. Say, "I'm really glad you got in touch with me. Listen, do you mind if I ask what prompted your call?" This is very important! No sale exists in a vacuum, and you have to know exactly what you're dealing with. Don't succumb to the temptation to sell—it may be too early.
3. Ask to set up an in-person appointment. Yes, even if the person tries to close the sale himself on the phone. You need to establish a personal bond.

Don't assume you've got a sure thing. Sales is a numbers game. Your objective is to turn the odds in your favor in as many different ways, and on as many different occasions, as humanly possible.

If you do that over the long haul, it will pay off handsomely.

Sales Technique #13
Listen, Learn, and Lead

It's important to lead your customer to where you (ideally) both want to go. But that raises the question, why would anyone want to follow you?

The reason is simple: it's because you are a leader. The best salespeople are.

A number of things factor into sales leadership. One of the most important is product knowledge. You know your product or service better than anyone else on the planet. You know how to adapt your products to fill a variety of your customers' needs. You know your pricing structure. You can make a deal that the customer can afford and that still allow you a good profit.

And, most important of all, you demonstrate your willingness to walk the extra mile. I think it was Groucho Marx who said concerning honesty and fair dealing, "Once you can fake that, you've got it made."

I don't subscribe to that notion. There's really too much at stake here, including your livelihood. And, quite frankly, if you can't genuinely be honest, if you don't really care about your customers, you should consider another line of work.

Caring, trying to do what's best for everyone involved, is an important leadership tool, one that will get a prospect to follow all the way to a signed contract. The key is to get as much information as you can.

Therein lies what I call the Power of Twelve. Here's how it works.

One of your leadership skills is knowledge. No one knows your product lines as well as you do. Now your goal is to reach that same level of knowledge about your customer. In order to fully understand the prospect's company and its needs, you need to see as many as twelve people in the organization.

Spend time with a buyer. Spend time at the manufacturing plant to see the way the people on the line make their products.

Spend time with the marketing staff to see how and to whom they sell their products. Speak to the company's sales force, its executives. And at every stop, ask all the people you meet how and why they do what they do and whether there's a way your product can help them do it better.

By the time you're through, you should know more about the company than its CEO. To do that, you have to listen to what they say.

When I asked a rep how many people were involved in making decisions on purchasing the nearly 400 products he sold to a company, he told me 200. When I asked him how many he called on regularly, he told me four.

How could he possibly sell to any depth if he only listened to and learned from four of 200 people? When I reviewed his efforts, it soon became clear to me that all he received were superficial orders. There was a lot of money (and commission) left on the table because he didn't follow this basic principle of the Power of Twelve. So he couldn't listen, he couldn't learn, *and* he couldn't lead.

Sales Technique #14

Read Industry Publications

Quick! What kind of people read *American Highway Engineer*?

How about *Publishers Weekly*? What audience subscribes to *Adweek*? Or to *Billboard*? Or to *Variety*?

These publications, and hundreds more like them, may be the most important documents you can get your hands on. The industry or industries you work in almost certainly have some sort of trade journal, magazine, or e-zine read by just about anyone of any consequence within the field. You can put yourself at a distinct competitive advantage in comparison with many salespeople by becoming familiar with these publications. Use them to keep abreast of industry trends. You should understand and be able to adapt to the business environment faced by your customers.

In addition, leaders of industry, in increasing numbers, are publishing blogs and offering webinars to explain their opinions about just about anything. The Internet is a rich source of cutting-edge information.

You will probably find that you can get a much better understanding of the technical jargon employed in your target group by reading articles written by people who actually work in the industry. Of course, you may have some trouble with a few of the denser articles aimed at subgroups within an industry, but you're much better off puzzling things through now than nodding your head vacantly when the terms are rattled off later!

The "who's who" or "on the move" sections of industry news websites can be a particularly fertile source of sales leads. On these sites, you will find the names and company affiliations of people who have recently been promoted or hired at a given company. Who wouldn't be flattered by a brief note of congratulations on having appeared on such a site—followed up by a phone call a few days later to talk about your company's product or service?

Sales Technique #15

Make a New Plan for Each New Prospect

It may be routine for you, but the prospect you're dealing with has never gone through the sales cycle with you before. One of the best ways I know of to combat that "here I go again" sensation is to produce a customized, written plan for your prospect. This should be based on the material you gather in your notes during the first and subsequent meetings.

After a while, you become familiar with certain objections or problems, and it's all too easy to pigeonhole your prospect. "I know that one; that's just like the problem the guy at ABC Company had." Well, it is and it isn't. It is not like the ABC problem in that the person who just outlined it has nothing to do with ABC Company, and he probably faces a number of different challenges related to the problem he just brought up.

A prospect who offers up an objection is really making a gesture of good faith. That may sound a little bizarre, but it's true. By taking the time to share a concern or problem with you, your prospect is passing along important information, key facts on the way your product or service needs to be adapted. Listening is the first part of the secret, and identifying the mutually accepted solutions is the second part.

Find out what those challenges are, and discover the unique circumstances or background your prospect may face. Then commit the solutions to paper, working with your prospect to determine the outline of the plan that will make the most sense in the current situation.

As a salesperson, you're like a doctor. It doesn't matter how many patients you've seen before. This one is the only one you're seeing now. Like the best doctors, you should make an effort to include the patient in your diagnosis and treatment. Doing so not only makes for a better working atmosphere, it also increases the likelihood that your patient will have the positive attitude that is really the driving force behind so many dramatic recoveries!

Sales Technique #16
Find a Compelling Opening Statement

When you try to get the person's attention, remember that people respond in kind. Salespeople tend to forget this, so they try a nifty opening such as, "If I could save you eight zillion dollars, would you be interested?" How do you feel when someone asks you a question like that?

Gimmicky openings don't work because they produce a gimmicky response. Ask a stupid question, and you'll get a stupid answer. If you ask a reasonable question or make a reasonable statement, on the other hand, you're going to get a reasonable answer. *People respond in kind.*

I got a call recently from a stockbroker. He said, "Mr. Schiffman, are you interested in investing in stocks?" I said, "No," because I wasn't. He hung up. End of call. I responded to the question in kind. Now, had he asked me, "Are you presently with a broker?" I would have said, "Yes," because I was with a broker, even though at that point I wasn't interested in reinvesting. But he would have had a conversation, and perhaps the beginning of a new relationship.

Another call I got recently went like this: "Good morning, Mr. Schiffman, this is XYZ Stock Brokerage House. We'd like to come over to your office and review your 401(k) plan for your company." I said, "Well, I'm really happy with what we've got." He said, "Okay," and hung up. That happens all the time! Ninety percent of all salespeople make that kind of telephone call.

I notice that a lot of the stockbrokers who call me try to keep me on the phone by saying, "Well, Mr. Schiffman, if I send you information, would it be okay if I call you back?" You don't need permission to call somebody back. That's foolishness. Just call the person back. If people don't want to take the call, they're not going to take the call. In fact, what most people who sell on the phone don't realize is that the first call is incidental. It doesn't really matter. It's the *second* call that will matter.

Don't talk fast or lie or mislead people to get appointments. I remember doing a program years ago for a company where the salespeople were taught to ask for the wrong name when making the cold call. If they were calling Bill Smith, they would say, "Can I speak to John Smith?"

Inevitably, the secretary or assistant would say, "There's no one here by that name. There's a Bill Smith." They say, "No, I want John Smith."

"There's a Bill Smith."

"Oh, then it must be his brother. Can I speak to him, please?"

So, Bill Smith gets on the phone because he can't figure out who would be calling him with the wrong first name. It doesn't make sense, especially if the name's a little bit odd. So he takes the call and immediately the salesperson says, "Oh, hi John," using the wrong name. Bill says, "No, this is Bill." "Oh, I'm sorry; you know something, I was looking at the wrong name. Anyway, let me tell you why I was calling." And then they get into their little script to see if Bill is interested in whatever they're selling.

The easiest, simplest way of opening up and getting the prospect's attention is by saying his or her name. Call up and say, "Good morning, Mr. Jones."

It's that simple. It's so simple it's almost scary.

The opening of your call is going to lead to a response. You can anticipate that response. You are then going to produce an appropriate turnaround, which should get the appointment. The key to the call is actually not the opening. The reality is no matter *what* you say in the opening, people are going to respond to you, and you can prepare for those responses.

Most people will respond positively to a positive-sounding call. Usually, if you speak politely and intelligently to people, they'll speak politely and intelligently to you. There will be a response in kind.

Sales Technique #17

Listen to the Prospect

Perhaps the easiest way to distinguish successful salespeople from unsuccessful ones is to watch how they interact with a prospect. Do they do all the talking, never letting the prospect get a word in edgewise? If so, it's a good bet you're looking at a failure.

You *must* let the prospect speak about himself or herself; the information you'll receive as a result is invaluable. Listening is the only way to target the product to the unique set of problems and concerns the prospect presents to us. By staying focused on the prospect (rather than "getting" the prospect), we build trust. And trust is vitally important.

When you get right down to it, a good salesperson doesn't so much sell as help. You can pass along important information and ask for the sale after you've demonstrated clearly how your product can help achieve an important objective—but ultimately, the prospect has to make the decision, not you.

Listening doesn't just mean paying attention to the words that come out of the prospect's mouth. Very little of what we actually communicate is verbal; most is nonverbal. Be sure you're "listening" in such a way that allows you every opportunity to pick up on nonverbal cues. By doing this—letting the prospect get across what's important to him or her—you'll stand out from the vast majority of other salespeople, who simply talk too much.

When your prospect wonders something aloud, give the person enough time to complete the thought. When your prospect asks you a pointed question, do your best to answer succinctly—then listen for the reaction. Allow the speaker to complete sentences—never interrupt. (What's more, you should let the prospect interrupt you at any time to get more information from you.) Express genuine interest in the things the prospect says. Keep an ear out for subtle messages and hints the prospect may be sending you.

When you do talk or make a presentation, keep an eye on your prospect to make sure what you're saying is interesting. If it isn't, change gears and start asking questions about the problems the prospect faces—you are probably missing something important.

Much of who you are and how you are perceived as a communicator—brash or retiring, open or constricted, helpful or manipulative—will be on display in a subtle but crucial manner in the opening moments of your first meeting with someone. Make sure you are sending the messages you want to send. Before the meeting, avoid preoccupations with subjects that have nothing to do with the client; these will carry over even if they never come up in conversation.

Always take notes during your meetings with prospects. As we'll see later, this dramatizes your attention and respect for the prospect's needs. (And if you think it's impossible to listen and take notes at the same time, you're wrong—the two actually reinforce each other.)

But what if the conversation is going nowhere? How do I listen if there's nothing to listen to? Shouldn't I make a pitch?

Probably not. The odds are that, early on in the meeting, you simply do not know enough about your prospect yet to go into a long presentation. So avoid doing that. Instead, focus your questions on three simple areas: the past, the present, and the future.

What kind of widget service was used in the past? What are the company's present widget needs? What does the prospect anticipate doing with regard to widgets in the future?

Add a "how" and a "why" where appropriate, and that's really all you need. Take notes on the responses you get.

After you summarize the points the prospect has made, you may be ready to talk in more detail about exactly what you can do to help solve the prospect's problems. But be sure that you listen first.

Sales Technique #18

Make Sure the Prospect Comes First

I don't think it's any accident that salespeople who experience high levels of success in their careers generally don't have to fake it through their discussions with customers and prospects. The stereotype of the salesperson may be the fast-talking used car salesman who manipulates people, but the reality is that people who do well in this profession don't come across as being eager to take advantage of anyone. They simply have a blast doing what they do for a living, and they genuinely enjoy talking about the pluses and the minuses of what they sell. They're sincere. They can be trusted.

I would rather see salespeople lose a sale because they were sincerely interested in the person's long-term interests than win a sale that subverts those interests. If they come to realize that this was the wrong product or service for them, it's better to be honest and to walk away than to make a sale that really does not help the prospect. That's what top-notch salespeople do, in my experience.

You have to have an underlying belief and sincerity in what you're saying in order to be successful. If you don't believe in what your organization is offering to consumers, go find somewhere else to work. If you don't believe in your ability to find the best answers for your prospects and customers, or you can't tell them the truth throughout the process, then you shouldn't be in sales!

Sales Technique #19

Understand the Prospect's Viewpoint

Get to know your product or service thoroughly, isolating how it helps people; only in this way can you apply your knowledge to the prospect's needs.

Salespeople usually know that they should outline product features: those constant, intrinsic elements the item presents. Someone selling a tin can might call attention to the fact that it's curved along the edges, and that it holds a certain amount of material. A fountain pen, in the same manner, can be said to have a point, or to write with ink. This book might be highlighted by pointing out that it's a certain number of pages long, or that it's rectangular.

All true. And all very boring.

Features are essential—no one wants to buy a fountain pen that does not have a point—but features are not usually the first thing on the prospect's mind. Typically, the prospect will be concerned with a different idea entirely: benefit. And this, too, must be emphasized by the salesperson.

Benefits are what the user will get out of an item. A tin can, when considered by a food-processing firm, might have a benefit if its design allows more cans of soup to be produced in a given day than the design of a competing can. Someone considering a fountain pen might isolate a benefit by noticing that one brand's ink cartridges are easier to load than another brand's. And someone comparing this book to another book on sales might notice that it's broken into brief, easy-to-read chapters—an important factor for a salesperson who's pressed for time.

What about your product or service? What benefits can you isolate? What tangible advantages do your customers have over the customers of the competition?

Once you begin to see things from this perspective—the potential customer's perspective—you'll be able to start assembling the key selling points of your product or service.

You should, if at all possible, actually use the product or service as a customer would. Research your product or service thoroughly from the prospect's point of view; isolate benefits. Then you'll be able to make crystal clear the advantages your prospect will have by choosing you.

Sales Technique #20
Make Fifteen Cold Calls a Day

There's a formula that's more important to successful salespeople than any other: A=P=S. Appointments give you Prospects give you Sales. If you have no new appointments today, what's your chance of getting a new prospect? It's nonexistent. If you have no new prospects, what's your chance of making a sale? That, too, is nonexistent.

The real question is, how many appointments do you need to generate one real prospect? Your appointment base is always going to be larger than your prospect base, which is going to be larger than your sales base. It's like a pyramid, with your appointments forming the base, your prospects forming the middle, and your final sales at the top.

For example, suppose that you don't make any new appointments today. You're not going to generate a new prospect. That means that, approximately eight weeks from now, you'll see no new sales. Now, you can argue with me and say, "People will call me." But that's not what we're talking about. We've already established that's going to happen; those are consumer-driven sales. We're talking now about how to get at that *last* third of all possible sales.

How many appointments do you need to get your prospects? How many phone calls does it take to get those appointments? If you don't know those numbers, how can you know whether your sales approach is working?

In my case, I know I need one appointment a day, or five new appointments a week. In order to do that, I have to call fifteen people each day. Fifteen times five gives me seventy-five. Over five days, I call seventy-five people; I generate five new appointments, which ultimately gives me my one sale every single week. And that's the objective.

Every single day that I'm not in front of a group, I still make fifteen calls. That's fifteen new people I haven't spoken to before. Even on busy days I still try to find a way to make those fifteen calls. On those days when I cannot reach anybody during normal business hours, I make calls starting at 7:00 A.M. I know the odds are that I will not reach people that early. But I also know that I will have fifteen messages out there, and at least one of those people will call me back.

I actually speak to seven of those people. For every seven people I speak to, I set up one new appointment. As a rule, I do that five days a week, so at the end of the week, I have five new appointments.

Now here's a trick question. If I make five new appointments this week, as I always do, how many total appointments will I have *next* week? Eight.

Why is it eight? Because I know for every five new appointments, I'm going back to three more for follow-through appointments. My closing ratio is: for every eight appointments, I make one sale. This means that I will bring in something in the neighborhood of fifty new accounts a year.

Cold calling is a numbers game (or, to be more precise, a ratios game). And this particular game *drives your sales*. How many calls do you make each day? Is it giving you the number of appointments that you require in order to be successful? How many appointments do *you* require to be successful?

You need to know your numbers and understand your ratios.

Sales Technique #21

Look at Your Numbers

Let me give you a series of numbers that I think are important: 293 > 149 > 49 > 83 > 10.

Now these are actual sales numbers. Let me tell you what they represent. A salesperson picked up the phone 293 times during a ten-week period. During that time, he spoke to 149 people and actually set up forty-nine first appointments. The eighty-three represents the total number of sales visits. Ten represents the number of sales. What these numbers tell you is that each week for ten weeks the salesperson went on an average of 8.3 appointments and made one sale.

Not exactly a major blowout in terms of numbers, but successful nonetheless. Why? Because this person *understood his numbers*. His goal was a new sale a week; he monitored his numbers and hit the goal.

I've said it before: sales is a numbers game. The fact is, every single time you pick up the phone you're getting *closer to a yes*. If you understand that concept, you'll be successful in sales.

Sales Technique #22

Call from a Script

Have you recently seen a movie or a television show that you really enjoyed? Sure you have. Did the actors in that drama or that comedy sound like they were reading from a script? No. It doesn't sound like a script because the actor has internalized what has to be said. That's what you must do. You have to internalize what you're going to say so it sounds natural.

I've been teaching a program on cold calling for years. I've learned it; I've memorized it; I've internalized it. I can, therefore, take that program and change or adjust it as the circumstances require. It always sounds natural.

The objective here is not to "handcuff" you with a script. The objective is to help you say what you need to say, while freeing you to pay attention to the prospect's response—that is what's really important.

What is the response? What is the person saying? Are we creating an atmosphere that will make it easy to make positive responses? Or are people responding negatively because we've asked the wrong questions, or asked the right questions in the wrong way? Using a script makes it easier for you to listen for crucial information, since you know exactly what you're going to say.

Sales Technique #23

Master Third-Party and Referral Calls

What I call the third-party endorsement approach to cold calling is very easy, and it may even complement the way you're now selling. This is the variation I use, and most of the salespeople I've trained say it's a very easy model to adapt.

The first thing to remember about this approach is that it uses the basic steps of all cold calling:

- Get the person's attention.
- Identify yourself and your company.
- Give the reason for your call.
- Ask for the appointment.

Start with the first step: *Get the person's attention.* I've already told you that the way you get the person's attention is not by saying something gimmicky (like, "Are you interested in making a million dollars?") but by saying the person's name. You can decide on your own approach here. Do you like to say, "Hi, Bob," "Hi, Joe," or "Hi, Jill"? Do you like to say, "Good morning, Mr. Jones"? Whatever you're most comfortable with, that's what you can use.

Now let's consider the second step: *Identify yourself and your company.* If I said to you, "This is Steve Schiffman from D.E.I. Franchise Systems, Inc.," the odds are you would not know who that is. So that statement, on its own, is not going to be entirely appropriate in getting an appointment or letting you understand who I am. I need to give you a chance to understand exactly what I'm talking about.

Why? Because when we telephone somebody, that person is not prepared for the call. We're the last thing on that person's mind.

We have to give them an opportunity to understand what we're talking about, and then paint a picture for them so they can visualize the process. Here's how to do that in my second step:

"This is Steve Schiffman, I'm the president of D.E.I. Franchise Systems, Inc. I don't know if you've ever heard of us, but we're an international sales training company here in New York City. I also have offices in Chicago and Los Angeles. I do a lot of work with . . ."

And now I mention the XYZ, the ABC and the 123 companies in the context of cold calling and prospect management. This is painting the picture. I said key words. I've said *sales training, cold calling, prospect management.*

Now you focus on a specific success story. You can choose your own references to call just about anyone you want to talk to.

A number of years ago I was working with a major bank. I had trained about 500 of their sales managers to be more effective on the phone. About six or seven weeks after completing the program, I decided that I'd call another bank. It occurred to me that, since one bank was doing something about sales, another bank would probably be trying to do the same thing. If I could help one bank do that better, I could help another. It really had nothing to do with the fact that the organizations were competitors. Once this approach crystallized in my mind, I realized *I had a means of entry into virtually any bank or financial services organization I wanted to call.*

The next day I took a directory, found the name of a senior vice president of another bank, called him up, and got a meeting.

Take a look now at the third and fourth steps.

Give a reason for your call and *Ask for the appointment.* Continue by saying, "The reason that I'm calling you today specifically is that I just completed a very successful sales training with the ABC Bank here in New York City. In fact, it increased their appointments by one-third. I'd like to stop by next Tuesday at three and just tell you about the success I had with the ABC Bank."

The beauty of this call is you never say, "What we did for ABC Bank will work for you." You're simply saying that you've worked with another company in this person's industry, and you were successful with that company. That's the heart of the third-party endorsement approach.

Now, what about referral calls?

You can use the referral call when you have called someone in the organization, and that person has referred you to someone else. This approach helps you make the most of that opportunity to get an appointment.

Now you already know that when you telephone somebody and that person says, "I'm the wrong person to speak with," you're not going to ask, "Okay, who's the right person?" Instead, you're going to say, "Oh, what do you do?"

This is where you have to be ready to think on your feet. Sometimes, you'll realize you really *are* speaking to the wrong person. Sometimes, you'll ask the person you're talking to for an appointment.

Assume you're able to confirm that you really are dealing with someone who is the wrong person. Assume too, that you ask your contact for the name of the right person to meet with. Usually the contact will say something like "Why don't you get in touch with Pete Smith."

Now use what you've already figured out. You call Mr. Jones; he tells you he's the wrong person. You get the name of the right person, then you call him. Call the right person and say:

"Hello, Mr. Smith. This is Jane Smith from XYZ Company here in New York. We're one of the top-three widget companies in America. The reason I'm calling you today specifically is that I just spoke to John Jones. He suggested that I give you a call to set up an appointment. I wanted to know if next Tuesday at 3:00 would be okay."

You don't need to go through a full explanation. All you need to say is that your referrer suggested you give a call to set up an appointment. If you follow the system I've set up, your statement will be completely aboveboard. You will have asked for the name of the *person you'd be meeting with.*

At some point in the conversation with Pete Smith you're going to get a reaction. The typical reaction is, "Oh? Why would he want me to meet you? Well, what's this about?" Of course, Pete Smith doesn't know anything about why you're calling.

You can then take a step back and say, "Well, the reason I called John initially was that I had just worked with the XYZ Company. We were very successful in training their salespeople to be more effective on the phone. And when I told him that, he said that I should talk to you to set up an appointment."

Now the person has to react. He can react by saying, "Well, we don't do anything like that." To which you're going to say (you know it already, right?), "Oh. So what do you do?" And no matter what he says next, you're going to say, "Well, you know something, we *should* get together. How about next Thursday at 3:00?" And now you've got the appointment, which is what you were after in the first place.

Sales Technique #24
Use Voice Mail Creatively

I'm always a little bit mystified when I run into salespeople who tell me they "don't believe" in voice-mail messages when it comes to making prospecting calls. Nowadays, that's a little bit like saying you don't believe in the planet Earth.

All the same, there are a good many salespeople we train who swear that it's a waste of time to leave messages for prospects. I have a sneaking suspicion that these salespeople simply don't like making prospecting calls in the first place. Reaching someone's voice-mail box is common. Excluding all those potential contacts is, I think, basically a rationalization for the bad idea of focusing your calling efforts on "warm calls" to people who are already familiar to you. The problem is, there usually aren't enough people in that category to support your revenue goals.

A huge number of decision-makers use voice mail to screen virtually all of their calls. Why would you want to simply hand that group of potential customers over to the competition?

I also talk to a lot of salespeople who take the opposite approach. They overcall cold contacts, and leave two, three, five, or even more voice-mail messages per week. All that time, effort, and potential annoyance for people who have not yet set any kind of Next Step!

This method of using voice mail is not only a huge waste of time, but also a poor way to initiate a business relationship. Think back on the last time you received three or more consecutive voice-mail messages in a single week from someone you didn't know. Were you more or less likely to return the person's calls at the end of the week?

Abusing voice-mail systems in this way can also lead you to distort your own calling numbers, and that can make identifying correct ratios and targets difficult. I can't tell you the number of salespeople I've worked with who've informed me that they make "fifty calls a week," but who actually make calls to just ten new contacts over a five-day period. They leave a message a day for each of those contacts, and consider each of those messages to be a separate call!

On the whole, I've found that good salespeople actually prefer delivering a solid, professional message to a voice-mail system, and dealing with the resulting return call. Here are five reasons for that.

1. The dynamic of the call is likely to be much more favorable, and a conversational tone will often be much easier to achieve.
2. When the person calls back, you're somewhat less likely to be interrupted (because you're less likely to be perceived as an interruption).
3. When the person calls back, he or she is more likely to actually listen to what you have to say.
4. You can easily leave messages for people who are difficult or impossible to reach directly on the phone.
5. You can make prospecting calls to voice-mail systems at just about any time of the day or night, which gives you more flexibility in scheduling.

In the age of voice mail, you must know how to leave a message that can increase your chances of having the person get back to you. I'm going to give you two specific, very effective ways to leave a message. The first way will give you between 65 and 75 percent return calls. The second way is almost 99 percent effective!

Let's say I'm calling someone, and the secretary or receptionist tells me I'm going to have to leave a message. My message will sound like this:

"This is Steve Schiffman from D.E.I. Franchise Systems, Inc.; my telephone number is 212-555-1234. Would you please tell him it's in reference to the XYZ Company?" Or, for a voice-mail system: "This is Steve Schiffman from D.E.I. Franchise Systems, Inc.; my phone number is 212-555-1212. It's regarding XYZ Company."

So when he or she calls me back, I'm going to say: "Oh, I'm glad you called me. The reason I called you is that we recently did a project with the XYZ Company."

And then I immediately go into my call about being successful with the XYZ Company. I have to carry that through. If I don't, then the calls will not be consistent.

You can't lie or mislead. You must leave your company's name as well as the referring company's. You must be precise, and you must make sure that the secretary or the assistant gets the name of your company. Be careful *not* to give the impression that you represent the XYZ Company. If you do that, you will have trouble later on. Maybe not on your first call or your second call, but eventually someone's going to say you misled them, and they'll be right.

The second method of leaving a message came to me in an interesting way.

Every once in a while, it's necessary to terminate someone; sometimes people just leave. That's just the way things go. Several years ago I had a representative working for me who didn't work out—I'm going to call him Bob Jones. After Bob left the company, I started thinking that, as president, I really should call everybody Bob had ever talked to in order to see whether I could start the conversation again.

The first company I called was a huge telecommunications company that Bob had met with; the headquarters were not far from our office in Manhattan. I asked to speak to the president of the company; the secretary got on the phone and said to me, "I'm sorry, he's busy. What's it in reference to?" Now remember, I usually say that my name is Steve Schiffman, my company is D.E.I. Franchise Systems, Inc., my telephone number is . . . and I go on to mention the referring company. But in this case, I had Bob Jones on my mind. I had been thinking about him for some time, because it was a little bit frustrating to me that he hadn't worked out. So I simply said that Bob Jones was my reason for calling. The secretary took the message.

About twenty minutes later, the president of the company called me back and said, "You had called me in reference to Bob Jones."

I said, "Oh, yes. Bob Jones worked for our company a number of weeks ago. He's no longer with us, and the reason I was calling you today is we've been very successful working with the ABC Bank. I'd like to stop by next Tuesday at 3:00 and tell you about our success with them."

He gave me the appointment, and we eventually started a business relationship.

I started thinking about that, about how many other people Bob had met with. And so I called everybody and nearly every single person—almost 100 percent—called me back. I used the same message every time, referring to Bob Jones. They virtually all called me back.

Sales Technique #25

Remember Why People Buy

I want to emphasize that the decision to buy from us in the first place does not happen out of thin air. It happens because the person decides to buy into our plan and use what we have to offer. Why would somebody do that? The answer is simple. They only choose to use what we sell if it makes sense to them to do so. Whether they call us up and ask us to come in and solve a problem, or we call them up and eventually make a presentation that they sign off on, the only reason the person ultimately decides to buy from us is that it really makes sense for them to do so—from their point of view. So what causes that decision to happen?

The answer in many cases is the proposal or plan or reason that we have given them for deciding to buy. If that reason is strong enough and compelling enough, and if we have elucidated it correctly, we are going to get the sale. If the reason that we give helps the person to do what he or she is already doing, we are going to get the sale.

But how do we get that reason or plan? Well, that goes to the step before the presentation. That is, the information-gathering stage. Notice that it is impossible to deliver a presentation that wins a sale if we do not have the information we need. In my training sessions, I emphasize the important point that one must, realistically, expect to spend 75 percent of the sales process in the information-gathering phase—notice how big that phase is in the model I have given you.

Nevertheless, it is a fact of life that we cannot simply barge into the prospect's office and begin asking questions. We must qualify or open the sale. That means developing a little bit of rapport, usually by means of some kind of small talk.

All four of these processes are interrelated, and each one must unfold out of the previous step. This is the microcosm of the sale. This is a map of what happens when we do not know someone and we turn them into a customer.

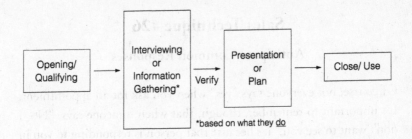

Sales Technique #26

Anticipate Common Responses

Of course, not everyone says "yes" when you ask for an appointment. It's important to remember, though, that when someone says, "No, I don't want to see you," it's because that person is responding to you in kind. He or she is responding to the question you posed. Don't think of this as an "objection." Think of it as what it is—a response to what you've just said.

You're soon going to realize that virtually every initial "no" response falls into one of these four categories:

1. "I'm happy with what I have."
2. "I'm not interested."
3. "I'm too busy."
4. "Send me some literature."

The trick is to learn how to anticipate and handle these responses properly.

"I'm Happy with What I Have"

I told you that your number one competitor is the status quo. This is true on two levels: First, the sales landscape is constantly changing, and you have to change with it. Second, for the most part, people really are happy with what they already have. The vast majority of the people you'll speak to will be happy, relatively "set." Otherwise, they would have called you. And guess what? They're not calling you!

You don't operate a business that's like a pizza parlor. People don't walk in and talk to you because they want to order something from you. You're reversing the process. You're out on the street, as it were, dragging people in for pizza!

I deal with a lot of banks. A number of years ago I called a bank at 7:00 A.M. and talked to a senior manager—the type who probably shows up at 4:00 A.M. The conversation went like this:

Steve: Mr. Jones, this is Steve Schiffman from D.E.I. Management Group. We're a major sales training company here in New York City, and we've worked with . . .

Mr. Jones: Steve, let me stop you right there. *(It's almost as if he held up his hand.)* We're already doing sales training. In fact, today's the first day of the program.

At this point, he held up the telephone so I could hear the noise of the people getting ready for the meeting. There I am at 7:00 A.M., listening to the sound of someone else starting a sales training session. How do you think I felt?

Mr. Jones: Can you hear? Phil's coming in right now!

I didn't know who Phil was. (I didn't even care who Phil was.) I listened, as I'd been instructed. Suddenly, it dawned on me. I shouldn't feel bad. I should feel great! This person has just told me he's a potential customer—he does sales training. So without missing a beat, I said:

Steve: You know something, Mr. Jones, that's great that you're using sales training. A lot of the other banks *(and I named several banks that we had worked with)* have said the same thing before they had a chance to see how our program, especially the cold calling program, would complement what they were doing in-house. You know something, we should get together. How about next Tuesday at 3:00? *(By the way, every word I'd said to Mr. Jones was absolutely true.)*

Mr. Jones: (After a pause.) Okay.

I got the appointment.

Think for a moment about how I did that. What I said was, in essence, "Other people told me exactly the same thing you did. They had the same reaction you did before they had a chance to see how what we do complements (fits into, matches, supports) what they're already doing. We should get together. How about next Tuesday at 3:00?"

In other words, I reinforced what Mr. Jones was already doing. I simply said that we could complement what he does, that we fit into that plan, that we could match that plan. I told him that he should look at our programs because of what he's already doing. I didn't tell him how to feel about the situation, or pretend I knew how he felt. I simply told him how I felt ("That's great!") and then told him the facts.

"I'm Not Interested"

Let's take a look at the next most common response. Let's say I call someone up and he says to me, "Steve, look, we're really not interested."

Here's what I say:

Steve: Well, Mr. Jones, a lot of people had the same reaction you did when I first called—before they had a chance to see how what we do will benefit them.

Isn't that the truth? Well, then say that. While you're at it, why not tell the person the names of the relevant companies you've worked with? If you have appropriate referrals, you should certainly use them, and this is the perfect time. Tell your contact that the XYZ Company, the ABC Company, and the National Widget Company all had the same reaction he did before they had a chance to see how what you do could benefit them. It's the truth.

"I'm Too Busy"

Typically, salespeople react to this by asking, "Well, what's a better time to call?" But in fact, this just kicks the can down the road. Mr. Jones told you to call back at 11:00 the next day to get you off the phone, not because he's serious about wanting to speak with you.

How can you get past this response?

Instead of asking, "What's a better time to call?" I say: "Mr. Jones, the only reason I was calling was to set an appointment. Would next Tuesday at 3:00 be okay?"

Look at what I just did. I took that first response, "Look, I'm too busy to talk," and responded with, "Oh—well the only reason I was calling was to set up an appointment." After all, you don't really want to have a conversation now!

You want to get the appointment. The truth is, the other person doesn't want to have a conversation now, either. The prospect, at this point, will raise another response, and you can deal with that. The point is, you've gotten past the "I don't have time to talk to you" problem.

"Send Me Some Literature"

This response is probably the most difficult to handle. The premise behind sending something is that the prospect will look at it, think about it, respond to it intelligently, and then when you call, you'll have an intelligent conversation about it.

Ninety percent of all salespeople will say that when they send material, it somehow doesn't get through to the person they mailed it to. Obviously that's not correct. You've got the prospect's e-mail address, and you attached the material to a cover letter and hit "Send." How could it not get through?

It got through. Your prospects just don't remember it. They don't care about it. They didn't read it. It doesn't really matter what happened to your material, does it? The point is that this approach doesn't move the sales process forward. It doesn't get you closer to an appointment.

Here's how to turn that response around. When the prospect says to you, "Look, why don't you mail me something?" just say, "Can't we just get together? How about next Tuesday at 3:00?"

It's as simple as that! "Can't we just get together? How about next Tuesday at 3:00?" Don't get any fancier than that. If you don't get the appointment, nine times out of ten, the person will say, "Well, I'll tell you the truth. I'm pretty happy with what we're doing." And you know how to respond to that!

Sales Technique #27

Show Enthusiasm

There is a difference between enthusiasm and poorly disguised panic. Enthusiasm builds bridges. Panic tears them down.

A sales meeting is like any other interaction. It takes a certain amount of time to get off the ground. If you understand the dynamics at work when you first come into contact with a prospect, you will go a long way toward understanding how enthusiasm must be conveyed as the relationship progresses.

When people meet someone new, they pass through a number of stages. There is among human beings a certain feeling-out process, an introductory stage. At this stage, because the two of you don't know each other well enough yet, you cannot convincingly say all that you might want to about solving the prospect's problem. The prospect—along with most of the rest of the adult members of our species—requires a certain "choosing" time before entering into a socialization stage with another person. So the best way to show enthusiasm in the very early part of the meeting is to underplay it. Confident bearing; good eye contact (but not to such a degree it could be confused with staring); a firm handshake; predictable, smooth movements as you walk from one point to another—these are the keys to communicating your excitement about the new relationship you're trying to build.

Only you can tell when the prospect enters the second stage of socialization, but rest assured that the change will be noticeable. It will be marked by a more relaxed, open approach, often reflected in less constricted body language. What you're looking for is the point at which the prospect listens not because he has agreed to do so, but because he wants to. Once you see that shift take place—and it may be during the first visit or during a subsequent one—you can change the "grammar" of your presentation.

You may decide to use your hands more in gesturing, or to use the prospect's preferred form of address ("Mr. Powers" or "Bill") somewhat more frequently. You might even feel comfortable using less formal phrasings and word choices: "Take a look for yourself." "How about that?" "And I'll tell you what we did."

Make an effort to avoid repetitive, mechanical gestures or responses. This is exactly what constitutes a less-than-spontaneous, unenthusiastic meeting. If your conversational partner insisted on constantly nodding his head up and down, with little real regard for what you had to say, how would you feel?

These are general guidelines; your individual interactions with prospects will vary because prospects themselves will vary. The point is that bolstering your presentation with appropriate enthusiasm (especially on the second and subsequent visits) is an essential part of good salesmanship.

Sales Technique #28

Tell Others Who You Are

Why not?

Why not tell your doctor? Your electrician? Your dentist? The cab driver you rode with this morning? Your friend at another company? The person you sit next to on the airplane? Your barber? Members of the community group or charitable organization you work with? The guy sitting next to you at the ballgame?

Why not make a point of broadcasting your profession to anyone and everyone—with pride? I'm not suggesting you subject everyone you know to a sales pitch, of course. What I am suggesting is that it become second nature for you to say, loud and clear, to every single person you meet, bar none, that you're a salesperson for XYZ Corporation, maker of the finest widgets west of the Pecos. Couple that with a handshake and a confident, look-you-in-the-eye smile, and you know what? Every once in a while, someone's going to say, "Widgets, huh? You know, we've been thinking about those . . ."

In my opinion, far too many salespeople have a pathological aversion to letting people know what they do for a living. The only reason I can come up with for this is that we often aren't quite as proud of what we do for a living as a brain surgeon might be, or an attorney, or an editor, or a scientist, or a teacher, or workers in any of dozens of categories who have no difficulty mentioning how they spend the majority of their waking hours.

We should be proud of being salespeople; I know I am! The economy of the society I live in would not function without people who do what I do for a living, and every transaction I undertake benefits all who are affected by it. Am I proud of that? You bet!

You should feel that way about your job, too. If you need to make some changes before you can feel that way, make the changes. Then look people in the eye and tell them what you do and who you do it for. Make it a habit. It may take a little work at first, but eventually you will begin passing along your name, profession, and company affiliation almost without thinking. (Here's a helpful hint: research indicates that a routine you stick with for twenty-one days will become ingrained and will become a permanent habit you can incorporate automatically.)

If you have to, start small and work your way up. You might begin by choosing friends or contacts you know well enough to talk to but who don't yet know what you do for a living. But the easiest route by far is to say what you do for a living and whom you do it for as you are introduced to someone. It's easier than you think, and it can pay tremendous dividends.

Sales Technique #29

Use Company Events to Move the Relationship Forward

It's part of the sales landscape—a law as dependable as gravity. No matter how effective, persuasive, or experienced a given salesperson is, some percentage of that person's promising leads will turn into "opportunities." These are static contacts that aren't moving through the sales process and can't be counted on to provide income—at least for the time being.

The question really isn't whether contacts will fall into the "opportunity" category but what steps to take when they do. How do you reignite interest and generate activity within your list of "cold" prospects? One approach is a strategy used by Canadian sales representative Gino Sette.

Gino decided to send an e-mail to every prospect who had decided *not* to buy from him over a given period. Basically, the e-mail said this: "It was a pleasure meeting with you a while back to talk about what your company was doing. Even though we were unable to move forward at that time, I'm still thinking about you."

Gino then invited each "cold" contact to sit in at one of his company's upcoming events. "This will give you an opportunity to evaluate firsthand how applicable what we do is to your business environment," he wrote. "Attached is a list of all upcoming training where my clients have approved outside observers. I've also included a brief description of each of the programs."

According to Gino, he got calls from prospects who were very interested in observing specific programs, even though they had initially declined his firm's services.

The e-mail strategy had another application as well. Gino decided to write to each member of his active client base and extend the same invitation. The message began as follows: "First of all, let me thank you for allowing us to work with you and XYZ Company. We are very excited to have you as part of our client list, as you are a significant player.

It is for this reason that I would like to extend the following invitation to you . . ."

As his flurry of return calls proved, Gino's innovative technique is an effective way to win back (or solidify) your position on the to-do lists of your customers and inactive leads. His idea can be adapted to training programs, open houses, media events, and any number of other occasions.

Sales Technique #30

Get Prospects to Open Up to You

"I can't seem to get prospects to open up to me during face-to-face meetings," a salesperson said to me. "Is there a simple way to encourage them to start talking during the information-gathering phase?"

"Yes," I replied. "Pull out a yellow legal pad and a pen, pose a question, and then look away from your prospect—and look thoughtfully at the pad. Wait to see what happens."

What you will almost invariably find is that the simple act of writing down the date and company name will cause the person to open up to you. The same basic strategy applies if you're selling over the phone. Say something like, "Hold on a minute, I want to write that down," or "Just a second, let me pull out my pad so I can get this all down." Letting the prospect know that you are preparing to take notes, and riding out the small silence that may follow, virtually always leads to detailed answers to your questions.

Again—you can't make things happen in the sales relationship if you don't know what the prospect is trying to accomplish. And you usually can't find *that* out unless the prospect receives nonthreatening "talk to me" messages from you during the meeting. My experience is that the very best way to send those messages is by pulling out a pad and taking notes. Here's what you're telling her or him by taking notes:

1. "You are in control of this conversation." (You're offering a good question now and again, but the prospect's response is what's driving the discussion.)
2. "I am focused like a laser beam on finding out what you do." (As opposed to being totally focused on, say, figuring out how to operate a PowerPoint demonstration.)
3. "I am organized." (How many of the people your prospect runs into during the course of the average day go to the trouble of recording important instructions in permanent, hard-copy format?)

4. "I am trustworthy." (Tactful, engaged note taking has a remarkable way of encouraging prospects to elevate you to informal "insider" status.)
5. "I consider you a 'big shot.'" (Hey—this person will determine whether or not you get a commission. If that doesn't equal "big shot," nothing does.)

There's another advantage to taking notes, of course: When you do so, you can use your pad as a tool for sketching out your own diagrams and ideas relevant to your prospect's situation.

Sales Technique #31

Give Speeches to Civic and Business Groups

Public speaking rates high on humanity's list of common fears. Yet I'm going to suggest that you take the time to develop your skills as a speaker and get out and share your (unparalleled!) expertise in your field with audiences—and not just audiences of people in your industry. Just about any audience, believe it or not, will do the trick.

There is a double-edged sword at work here. First off, you will benefit tremendously from the boost in confidence you receive from being treated as an expert in your field. By the way, if you don't consider yourself an expert in your field, you shouldn't be selling in it. Your customers are certainly counting on your expertise!

Think about it. You know your subject. You talk about it all day long. Once you can make the minor adjustment of being able to give a lecture about what you do, you'll be a lecturer. Get someone to note you, and you'll be a "noted lecturer." Pretty soon, there may well be a lot of people noting you. Then you'll be a "widely noted lecturer." And deservedly so!

The second benefit to you of public speaking is even more remarkable. Studies have shown that when salespeople and consultants give speeches, on average, about one in ten audience members will seek out the speaker afterwards to ask about his or her services. What this really means is that 10 percent of any given audience you talk to will end up qualifying itself—and entering your prospect cycle! Who knows what might happen if you actually took the initiative to shake some hands and pass out business cards during intermissions and at the event's conclusion?

Where to go to give the speech? Well, outside of the channels that may exist in your industry (such as addressing a trade conference or taking part in an annual convention), consider contacting your chamber of commerce about local round tables. Other possibilities include your area's Rotary Club, Kiwanis Club, or any group that seems relevant to the economy of your community or tied in somehow to what you do.

Go to the club or organization you've targeted, state your case, and see what happens. More often than not, they'll be glad to work you into the schedule.

So ask yourself, "What have I got to lose?" Absolutely nothing! If it doesn't work out, at least you've made an effort—and gotten your name out in front of that many potential prospects. Give public speaking a try. Believe me, more than one salesperson has benefited tremendously from taking this route!

Sales Technique #32

Ask for Referrals

My favorite story about referrals has to do with a very successful sales-person I know named Bill. Every year he vacations in some exotic locale like Fiji or the Cayman Islands or Hawaii. Often, these vacations come as a result of company bonuses for his performance or industry awards. So about once a year, Bill sends an e-mail to his customers and quali-fied prospects announcing his return from paradise, where he received the XYZ Award for Outstanding Salesmanship. Bill's purpose is to thank his clients for their business and to make it perfectly clear that the only way he has been able to attain his goals is by helping custom-ers attain theirs. Classy, yes?

At the end of the message is a paragraph that runs something like this: "As you know, my business depends upon referrals. I would very much appreciate it if you would take a moment now to jot down the names and phone numbers of three or four people in the industry you feel might benefit from talking to me. Of course, if you do not wish me to use your name when contacting these people, all you have to do is indicate this in the space I've provided below. Again, thank you for your business, and here's to continuing success for both of us." Call me crazy. But I have a feeling there may be some cause-and-effect connection between letters like that and all those expensive vacations and impressive sales awards.

Let's play a little multiplication game. Suppose five people give you five referrals each, for a total of twenty-five. Of those new referrals, suppose that 60 percent turn around and give you five referrals, too. That's fifteen times five, or seventy-five new prospects. Now, of those seventy-five, let's say another 60 percent gives you five referrals each . . . you get the picture. If you're out to build your client base exponentially (and why wouldn't you?), you'll have trouble finding a better place to start than asking for referrals.

Referrals are the lifeblood of a successful career in sales. And yet salespeople are usually terrified to ask for them.

Often, they feel it will somehow threaten the relationship they've built up with a customer to ask about other associates who might benefit from their product or service. Perhaps the customer really doesn't like using the product or service after all, and asking for a referral will only intensify that feeling or bring it to the surface.

Conservatism is one thing. Paranoia is another.

Make Referrals Work for You

How can you make referrals work for you? Let's say your goal is to get five new prospects for the week. Carry with you at all times a package of three-by-five index cards. After you're done meeting with one of your customers or a good-quality prospect, simply say something like this.

"Mr. Jones, I'm willing to bet there are people in your (industry, area, related businesses) who could benefit from my talking to them about this (product/service)."

As you say this, you take out five index cards. Hold them in your hand. Let the prospect or customer see that there are five of them there. Then say, "Do you know five people I could talk to?"

Help your contact along. It will be easier than you think; the fact that there are five separate index cards will make the task comprehensible and immediate. Your confident, professional attitude will guarantee that your request will not be seen as inappropriate.

Put the cards in a row on the desk as you fill them out, writing names only. Then, after you have identified the five referrals by name, go back and ask for the company affiliations, addresses, or other contact information. You do this because you want to make the first and most important job, identifying the people you can talk to, as easy as possible.

Sales Technique #33

Be a Messenger of Change

There's a point in my seminars when I ask salespeople, "Who's your number one competitor?" Of course, they name every company they can think of that's offering a similar product or service. And they're all wrong. The fact of the matter is, as I said in the introduction, the number one competitor that every single company faces is the status quo.

As we've seen, the key objective of selling is asking people what they do, how they do it, when they do it, where they do it, who they do it with, and why they're doing it that way. And then our job is to help them do it better. But in order to help them do it better, we actually have to become messengers of positive change. Successful salespeople are prepared to do that, day in and day out.

In order to be successful at selling, you're going to have to get someone to change what he's doing now, to work with you instead of following the path of least resistance. Are you ready for that?

How do you pull something like that off? First and foremost, you have to know your product or service very well. (In other words, you have to be comfortable actually using it, just as a customer would.) And number two, you have to be convinced, deep down, no kidding, that your product will, in fact, help people. Finally, you have to be versatile enough to adapt your product or service to whatever it is the customer is trying to do. This assumes, of course, that you're willing and able to listen to the customer long enough to find out what he or she is trying to do!

Not long ago, I was teaching a course in a high school about sales. (Yes, believe it or not, there are people in high school who are interested in careers in sales!) At the conclusion of one class, I was asking the students to tell me what they'd picked up from this initial discussion that we had about sales. One young man raised his hand and said to me, "Mr. Schiffman, the one thing that I've learned today is that you aren't as important as what the customer is all about; you have to say to yourself, 'The customer is really more important to me than anything else.' And what it is they want to do, what they are trying to accomplish, and how they want to do that is much more important than your product or anything that you have to say."

He was absolutely right. A superior salesperson has to accept that: there's no lecturing prospects or customers, no reading from brochures, no memorized monologues. None of that is as important as asking, "Hey, what are you trying to get accomplished here?" and then listening for the answer that comes our way. Once we hear that answer, once we can respond intelligently with suggestions based on our own product knowledge, then we're in a position to help bring about positive change. Not beforehand!

PART III

MAKING THE SALE

When the rubber hits the road and you're sitting in a room with your client, your presentation, and a dryness at the back of your throat as you get ready to start, you're probably thinking that this is what selling's all about—actually talking to the client.

That's true, but it's also part of a process. And, as you'll see in this section, all the bits and pieces of the process have to work in harmony for the sale to be successful. A good sales call is about preparation as well as execution.

Sales Technique #34

Plan Your Day Efficiently

Committing to a daily schedule is of paramount importance; your success or failure in this area will have a major impact on your overall performance as a salesperson.

Here are some tips on tightening your day and making it productive.

- Don't waste hours you could be speaking with clients. Plan your day the evening before.
- Prioritize your goals. Don't just start filling out a schedule willy-nilly one evening; make a list of all the things you want to accomplish, then rank them in the order of their importance before you include them on your schedule.
- Leave time for crises. Scheduling every day to the brim will cause you to slip from your plan. We all know that strange, unpredictable problems have a way of cropping up from time to time. Leave an hour or so open at the end of the day to manage sudden difficulties. If no crisis arises, you can always move on to your next priority item.
- Get up fifteen minutes earlier than you do now—and give yourself a positive charge of energy in the extra time. Starting the day in a rush gets things off to a bad start. Begin the day with a positive affirmation: "This is going to be a great day." Eat a good breakfast. Listen to pleasant music. Stay away from reading or listening to the news first thing in the morning; it's too depressing. Be nice to yourself. (Don't worry; it won't last long.)
- Buy and use a doctor's appointment book—the kind with the whole day marked off in fifteen-minute increments. Then keep close watch on the time you spend on any given item. This approach will help you avoid the temptation to allocate vast chunks of your day to vaguely defined goals when you assemble your to-do list.

Also buy a second, smaller book—one that can fit in your pocket or purse. Here you will record what you actually do during the day.

Nothing extravagant, just a quick jot-down of the time for each project you undertake as you work through the day. The beauty of this is that you end up with a written record of events, not just your plans, and you can compare the two at day's end. If there's a huge discrepancy between what you plan at 6:00 P.M. on Tuesday and what you've actually done by 6:00 P.M. on Wednesday, you'll know about it and be able to work on it.

- On Friday evening, prepare not only your Monday morning schedule, but also your thumbnail sketch of the week to come. Odds are that this will take the form primarily of meetings and other commitments; don't feel you have to account for every minute of every one of the next five days. Just block out your scheduled appointments and meetings so you have a good solid overview of what's on the horizon. Where appropriate, leave yourself "into-and-out-of" time. After all, you know that you won't simply materialize out of thin air at your three o'clock appointment across town, but will have to drive there, leaving early enough to assure arrival ten minutes or so before three.

By attending to daily scheduling matters conscientiously, and comparing your actual results with your plan, you'll increase your time-effectiveness and lay solid foundations for your sales success.

Sales Technique #35

Get Organized!

Your professional image depends to a large degree on your personal appearance. However, you should keep in mind that it also depends on your tool.

What do you suppose goes through the mind of a prospect who, upon meeting a salesperson, sees all sorts of objects tumble randomly from his or her opened briefcase?

Your briefcase should give the impression of order and precision when opened. It should not be overflowing with laundry lists, last week's newspapers, dirty ties, bills, or food.

It should contain: your legal pad; your business cards; your pens; appropriate product materials and/or samples; a handheld calculator; and perhaps your pocket-sized datebook. That's it.

Often, salespeople will bring too much to an appointment. You don't need everything in the building to talk to a single prospect, and even though carting along reams of samples and brochures may make you feel more secure on the way to the appointment, you're likely to look confused and befuddled as you paw through it all trying to find the material you want.

Stay away from the fancy flipcharts and display boxes and framed testimonials. They're virtually always more trouble than they're worth. Usually, the only thing you can count on from all this extraneous materials is a less confident, poised presentation.

If you find that you're going to your appointments so weighed down with samples and display cases that you're exhausted from the minute you walk in the door, you will eventually have to make a change somewhere. If it's agony for you to carry all that, it will be agony for the prospect to look at you. Try to pinpoint the prospect's areas of concern; you can always bring requested material on your second visit.

As we will learn a little later in this book, business can be compared, in many respects, to war. Both require strategy, planning, competition, intelligence, and so forth. If you think of your sales work in that way, you'll see that your sales tools are really part of your ammunition. As such, they should be maintained with care and respect.

Sales Technique #36

Don't Product Dump

A salesman told me, "I give what I think is a great opening summary of my company and its products and services during the opening phase of the first meeting. It takes fifteen to twenty minutes. Prospects don't seem to be responding well to it, though. What's happening?"

"What's happening," I replied, "is you're forgetting one of the most important facts of professional sales: *You are more than a walking brochure!*"

Most salespeople are taught to "find the needs" of their prospects, so they can make presentations designed to show how their organizations can fill those "needs." In fact, they get used to six or eight common "needs" and become very comfortable indeed discussing them.

There's a problem with this approach, though. It turns you into a walking advertisement. You recite a familiar "spiel" during your first meeting. Guess what? The odds are high that your prospect already has—or has access to—some variation on what you offer. He or she doesn't really "need" you at all.

The act of reciting a well-known (and lengthy) monologue to a prospect is called, executing a "product dump." It means we are sending far more information *out* during the first meeting than we are taking *in*. In fact, product dumping is the most common reason for a first meeting with a prospect *not* to go well. Prospects hate hearing a product dump during the first meeting.

In assessing people's needs, we usually assume we know all about their business already. We assume that this prospect is facing exactly the same situation as the last prospect we met with. So we just soliloquize about what we have to offer or read from a brochure. In so doing, we overlook opportunities to gather meaningful information about what's actually going on in the life of the person we're talking to. The result: another turned-off prospect.

The reason so many salespeople rely on product dumps is that meetings with prospects can be stressful. When we're stressed, we fall back on what's familiar to us—namely, what we know about our product or service. Unfortunately, when we do that, we close down the lines of communication.

Not long ago, I had a visit from a salesperson who represented a copier company. The meeting consisted of a brief exchange of greetings, a couple of superficial remarks about the weather and the traffic, and the salesperson's spiel about the features of his machine. This spiel went on, uninterrupted, for twenty minutes, at the conclusion of which time the fellow tried to "close" me. He didn't succeed. He tried again. He didn't succeed. He packed up his things and left.

Why do I share this story with you? Because I want you to understand the real reason I didn't even consider buying from this young man. *He never asked me what business I was in.*

Don't try to sell that way. Don't let your nervousness shut down the possibility of learning the most elementary facts about the person you're talking to. Don't miss out on a chance to find out a little bit more about your prospect than that stressed-out copier salesperson did.

Sales Technique #37

Know Your Objective

You've made the call. You've gotten the appointment. You're walking into the prospect's office for the first time. What is it, exactly, that you're trying to accomplish?

As it happens, there are two goals you should bear in mind as you initiate the first person-to-person contact.

Goal Number One: To send concise but unmistakable symbols of professionalism and accountability. To offer, in short, a brief self-identification message that avoids the trap of self-obsession, and that sends without any countervailing signals the message, "It is good business to do business with us."

Goal Number Two: To listen.

Note, please, that presenting the product or service is not a goal at this stage of the sales cycle! You don't know enough yet about your prospect's problems to propose a solution to them.

Selling means asking people what they do, how they do it, when they do it, where they do it, why they do it, and whom they do it with—and then helping them do it better. That's precisely what you should begin to do in your first meeting.

That doesn't mean you manipulate your conversation with the prospect. It means you artfully steer that conversation into areas of mutual opportunity.

In the sample dialogue that follows, notice how we send the "good-business-to-do-business-with-us" message early on, and then gently steer the prospect toward the questions regarding the past, the present, and the future. By the way, in all such encounters, you should always be sure to take written notes based on the information you get from your prospect.

You: (after engaging in small talk) Mr. Prospect, would it help if I told you about me and my company first?

Mr. Prospect: Yeah, why don't you do that?

You: Okay. We've been in business for the last six months (two years, ten years, 200 years, whatever), and we happen to be the most dynamic widget company in the country. We've worked with companies like ABC Financial, DEF Communications, and GHI Printing, and we've worked with each of them to develop a customized widget system that worked for their specific needs. Today I was wondering if we could talk a little bit about your company's widget plans.

Mr. Prospect: Shoot.

You: Okay. Have you ever worked with a widget company before?

Mr. Prospect: Well, yes, once we did, back in 1979.

You: How did it work out?

Mr. Prospect: Hmm . . . I can't recall any problems with it whatsoever, to tell you the truth. A couple of years after that, of course, we had some budget cutbacks; you know how it is . . .

You: So presently you're not using anything in this area?

Mr. Prospect: That's right. It comes up every now and then at board meetings, but there never seems to be enough of a reason to reconfigure the entire department's production equipment. So it usually gets tabled. My feeling is that a good widget system here could be worth looking at, though.

You: Okay. Now, I'm curious. Does your production department foresee about the same level of work in the next six to twelve months as it's doing right now? Or more? Or less?

Mr. Prospect: Funny you should ask about that. I was just talking to Roger Gardner over in production this morning, and he's a little concerned about how they're going to meet the targets for the next two quarters.

And given that information, you should continue to steer the conversation into the specific hows and whys of the situation at Mr. Prospect's production department.

Sales Technique #38

Master PIPA

Sometimes I hear from salespeople, "I don't know how to handle the transition out of the 'small talk' phase of the meeting. What's the best strategy?"

I've developed a sequence to help you out here: Present, Interview, Present, Agreement (PIPA). This PIPA outline can produce spectacular results for you from the very first moments of your initial meeting with the prospect. Let's see how the sequence works at the beginning of a meeting.

The PIPA Sequence: Roadmap for Great Conversations

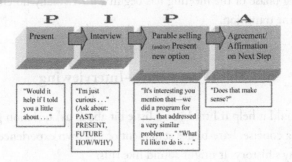

As a matter of social convention, "icebreaker" questions—questions that help you build rapport and a sense of commonality with the other person—are likely to begin your meeting. Even these kinds of questions can be pointed in a direction that illuminates your prospect's unique situation. For instance:

"I'm just curious, how does someone get to be a (Vice President of Widget Reclamation/Senior Data Analyst/CEO/etc.)?"

Once you have completed this small talk portion of your initial meeting, you will be ready to make a seamless transition into the "business" segment of the meeting. The first "P" in the PIPA sequence will help you do just that.

The First "P" in PIPA—Presenting

After the brief "get-acquainted" portion of the meeting draws to a close (usually indicated by a sizable pause), direct the meeting toward the business at hand by asking something along the following lines:

"Mr. Prospect, would it help if I told you a little bit about our company and what we do?"

By doing this, you are *presenting* an option—that is to say, implementing the first "P" in the PIPA sequence. (Important note: It's *not* an excuse for a product dump.)

In the unlikely event that the prospect tells you he or she *doesn't* want to hear about what you and your company do but has something else pressing to discuss, simply follow the prospect's lead. The information-gathering phase of the meeting has begun with virtually no effort from you on the transition.

The "I" in PIPA—Interviewing

The "would it help if I told you a little bit about us" question points us toward a concise, bare-bones statement of our own experience and the company's history. It might sound like this:

"Well, ABC Widget Development is the largest specialized widget manufacturing company in the United States. We've been in business since 1923, and I've been working for the company as a senior account representative since 1997."

Now *immediately* pose a question that meets three qualifications:

1. It focuses on what the prospect does.
2. It focuses on some broadly defined area where we have added value for other customers.
3. It is likely to be easy for the prospect to answer.

The moment we pose this "do-focused" question in an area in which we feel we can add value, we are seamlessly making the transition into the second, and most important, part of the PIPA sequence—*gathering information*. So we would conclude our "little bit about us" statement by saying, "Mr. Prospect, I'm just curious, have you ever worked with a custom widget manufacturer before?" and let the interview flow from there.

The Second "P" in PIPA—Present a Next Step Option

Once you have gathered enough information to get a sense of where the relationship should go next, you'll be in a great position to use the second "P" in PIPA. You will present a next step recommendation.

It could sound like this:

"Based on what you've told me today—specifically X, Y, and Z—I think I should put together a preliminary proposal to give you an idea of what we might be able to do for you in this area. Why don't I come back here next Tuesday at two o'clock?"

Always ask for a next step that's easy, logical, and helpful and that's connected to a specific date and time. Make the subject of your conversation *when* you'll be meeting next, not *whether* you'll be meeting next. See what happens!

The "A" in PIPA—
Agreement That Your Next Step Makes Sense

It's not enough simply to present a next step option. In the "A" portion of the PIPA sequence, you make sure that the other person specifically agrees to the step you have proposed.

Your prospect may agree immediately with the next step you suggest. Then again, he or she may offer a confusing or uncertain response. When this happens, you will want to tactfully but firmly move the issue to the forefront by exploring whether or not what you've suggested *makes sense*.

The best way to find out about this is simply to ask: "So—do you think it makes sense for us to get together again at this time next week?"

The beauty of this approach is that if it *doesn't* make sense to the other person, he or she will usually explain *why* it doesn't!

If the person doesn't provide any information about why the next step you've proposed doesn't make sense, use the "I didn't anticipate that" technique outlined below.

You: So—do you think it makes sense for us to get together again next Tuesday at two o'clock?

Prospect: I'd really rather not.

You: I'll be honest—that's a surprise to me. I didn't anticipate that you'd say that. Usually, at this stage of the meeting, when we find out about X, Y, and Z, people are eager to learn what happens next, and they want to set up a time to do that. Did I do something wrong?

Prospect: Oh, no—it's nothing you did. The problem's on our end. You see, the thing is . . .

Those are the magic words: "The thing is . . ." Now you're going to hear more critical information. Be sure to take careful note of anything and everything that follows the words "The thing is"! This information is likely to be extremely important.

Sales Technique #39

Communicate Trust

I've trained over a half-million salespeople. And the more salespeople I run into, the more exposure I get to various "tricks of the trade"—little corners salespeople cut in order to get ahead (or so they think) over the short term. The only problem is, too many of these "tricks of the trade" undercut an essential objective: that of constantly sending and reinforcing the message that it is a good business decision to trust you.

I know a car dealer who finds a random name of someone in his area, calls the person, and says, "Hi, Mr. Jones, this is Mike Johnson at Johnson Used Cars. You've just won our raffle! Come on in and collect a turkey!" What he never says is that he really wants the person to come in and collect two turkeys: one to put in the oven, and the other for the driveway. (By the way, there is no raffle; the turkeys are bought as premiums for anyone who walks through the door.)

The successful salesperson makes a *good leader* because he or she inspires trust. I think that the truly successful salespeople today—and, by the way, this is what I see in world-class sales forces—have the personal magnetism and the self-assurance to say to people, "Follow me"—and thereby win long-term, happy customers. That kind of authority only comes with complete, unflinching confidence that you can deliver results for your prospect. If you're right, your customers trust you—and follow you.

Building trustworthiness, then, means *building leadership skills*. That's not to say you should practice railroading your customers! All the confidence and authority in the world won't change the I-found-that-wallet-you-never-really-lost scam into a way to build trust. It means understanding your product or service, understanding what your prospects do for a living, and assuming responsibility for delivering results to your customers, no matter what. Prospects can sense when this is what you're offering, and they like it.

A good leader:

- Has a vision
- Commands respect
- Sees the big picture
- Knows when to change direction
- Points out problem areas and is ready to discuss solutions
- Has confidence in both approach and attitude
- Is accountable

All of these traits add up to true trustworthiness.

Too many salespeople focus on whether or not they *appear* trustworthy. That's not the point! You want to develop an earned reputation for following through on everything—and I mean every syllable—that comes out of your mouth. If you say you'll call at 9:00 A.M., then call at 9:00 A.M., and not 9:02 A.M. Better yet, call at 8:55 A.M. and be willing to be put on hold! Some salespeople take this principle and turn it into a recipe for annoyance; others display the spark of professionalism necessary to demonstrate dependability and consistency as personal hallmarks.

Such "minor details" have real persuasive power. At the beginning of your relationship with a prospect, those details are all he or she has to go on. They're the only tool you have! Spout lavish promises, and fail to follow through on the details, and you'll be like every other salesperson. But say you're ready, within the next five minutes, to fax or e-mail over a quote that completely meets all the prospect's specifications, then *do it* . . . and you're one in a million

You must demonstrate that you are unfailingly dependable in all things, big and small, and you must make a habit of delivering what you promised (or, preferably, more). Then you will be in a position to say with authority, "Follow me."

Sales Technique #40
Ask the Right Questions

Traditionally, salespeople are taught to ask about the pain, to ask about the problems associated with whatever's going on in the prospect's world. But in doing that, you actually limit yourself to a very small percentage of the situations where you could add value.

By asking about pain and problems, you limit yourself to winning sales from those people who are willing to answer "Yes" when you ask them if they have any problem or feel any pain. The rest of the people are going to be "All set." And that's what you're going to hear, over and over again. Some variation on, "We're all set."

Eventually, you'll realize what I realized after a few months of selling. The answers we get are directly related to the questions we ask. In other words, you and I as salespeople create the conversational flow during all our exchanges with all the people we talk to during the course of the day.

Let's say that I sit down across from your desk and say to you, "Mister Prospect, what pain are you having right now with your current vendors?" I'm going to get an answer based on the concept of "Pain." You might say, "This is the problem: we are feeling pain about so-and-so." And I might get some degree of business from you.

There's nothing wrong with this approach when you get the business, but a large percentage of the time, you're going to say to me, "Steve, we have no problems with our vendors. We're all set."

The other day a banker dropped by my office to talk to me. This particular banker has been coming to see me now for the last six years, trying to get my business. Every year, for six years, he calls up, sets an appointment, and then comes by my office and says, "Steve, are you having any problems with your bank?"

I always say, "No, things have been going pretty good for me."

And he says, "Well, you know, there's got to be something that's bothering you."

And I say, "No, not really."

I've been talking to him for six years, and he always leaves because he can't find a problem or pain. I'm always all set with my current bank.

Another Kind of Question

What if that banker had asked a different question altogether?

Suppose he had asked me something like this:

"Steve—just out of curiosity—how did you choose your current bank?"

If he'd asked me that question—a question based on what I had done in the past rather than what he thought my pain or problem was—then he would have gotten a very different answer, wouldn't he?

Instead of saying, "No, I don't have any problems," I would have said, "Well, I got a referral from a friend who spoke highly of the bank, and I saw that it offered a no-fee checking account, and that was interesting, so I went ahead and opened an account."

Which of these two approaches is more likely to yield a meaningful dialogue with the prospect?

1. What would you change about your current bank if you could change anything? (Attempt to "find the pain.")

   Or:

2. How did you choose your current bank? (Attempt to learn about what the prospect did, is doing now, or is planning to do.)

For most of us, our number-one competitor in the field is what the person you are trying to sell to is already doing. The number-one competitor is, as I've been saying throughout this book, the status quo. Very few of the people you are going to sit down with today, next week, next month, or next year are not already using some kind of product or service right now. In fact, they are all using or doing something—even if they are currently deciding not to use anything like what you offer.

You walk in there—and I don't care what you sell, whether you are selling banking, Internet access, training programs, paper, shipping, whatever—the fact is that every single person you are calling on is doing something right now. It may not be what you want them to be doing, and it may not be the way you want them to do it, but they are doing something. And it makes sense to them right now to do it that way.

Sales Technique #41

Give Credit to the Client's Intelligence

It's not uncommon to hear a salesperson say something like, "You know, the prospect I met with today was so dumb—he had no idea what I was talking about." Maybe you've even heard yourself making remarks like that.

What does that say about you as a salesperson?

You are a conveyor of information. You are a conduit. You are the connecting unit between your business and the end user. How can a prospect know the ins and outs of your business before you explain anything? And why, for that matter, should that prospect need to know more about your business than your phone number, anyway?

There is one area, though, that the prospect has a great deal of knowledge about—knowledge you need. And that area is his or her problems. Remember, solving customer problems is what sales is all about, and you will—or should—spend a great deal of time trying to ferret out information from your prospects.

Considering all that effort, it doesn't really make sense to proceed on the assumption that the prospect doesn't know anything. Clearly the prospect does know something important; otherwise you wouldn't set up meetings to try to learn that something.

Your job is to learn the problems the prospect is having, and then show how your product or service can be used to competitive advantage in solving those problems. You must approach this task as the prospect's partner and as an equal. If you bring arrogance or a superior attitude to the appointment, it will show through, and your sales will suffer.

The prospect doesn't know your product or service as well as you do because he or she doesn't sell it for a living. You do, and you should be able to provide essential information immediately, not shake your head in disappointment that the prospect isn't catching on as quickly as you'd like.

You can encourage the efficient flow of information between yourself and your prospect by being scrupulously honest with the prospect about your company and what it has to offer. Acting otherwise can cause big problems. I was working with a company that produces industrial machinery recently; one of their sales reps was indignant that her prospects had "lied" to her about the status of forthcoming orders. As it happened, this rep's whole approach to customers was flip, glib, and, on the whole, disrespectful. My guess is that she herself was not completely honest in dealing with her prospects. Is it any wonder she got bad information back from them?

As long as you and your prospect, working together, can define the problem to a degree sufficient for you to be of help, the prospect is quite intelligent enough. Your goal is not to dwell on what you consider to be the prospect's shortcomings, but rather to encourage an extremely intelligent decision: that of doing business with your firm.

Sales Technique #42
Beware of Bad Assumptions

A national sales manager I know was trying to expand his presence in one of his biggest accounts. He was not particularly successful, and he wanted my help in figuring out exactly why.

I asked him, "What are you selling them specifically?"

He said, "Well, among other things, paper—reams of business stock for use in copiers and printers."

I said, "Okay, how many people in the organization use paper?"

"Well," he said, "there are probably 15,000 people who use it, but there are only about 400 different work groups."

"Okay," I said. "There are 400 different work groups. How many of them are you talking to?"

He went on to explain to me that he was "pretty certain" that they all bought through a single channel—namely, his channel. "That, at any rate," he said, "is my assumption."

I asked, "Why are you so certain of that?"

There was a long pause.

"I'll tell you one thing," I said. "If I had a company with 15,000 people using paper, I sure as heck wouldn't be channeling every single solitary purchase decision through one guy. My guess is that there are a lot more channels where paper is being sold than you're taking into account here. Have you ever asked them how they acquire their paper for those 15,000 people and those 400 work groups?"

"Well, no," he said.

We all can fall into this trap. We want to assume that the guy that we are talking to really is the guy who controls everything. We want to assume that the way that we have established a relationship really is the most efficient way to interact with our prospects. We want to assume that the work that we have done up front really is the only relevant work for us to do. But, in so many cases, those assumptions are not warranted.

The one thing that you can be sure about, especially in a major account, is that there is something going on behind the scenes that you can find out more about. In this case, I'd ask, "Just so I can be clear . . . how exactly do you acquire paper for your 400 work groups and your 15,000 people?"

That is the kind of question that a CEO or a senior executive will usually answer with confidence and authority and complete forthrightness in about a tenth of a second. By the same token, it is the kind of question that somebody who is placed a little bit lower on the chain of command would probably avoid, or he or she might spend forty-five minutes describing your terms back to you. So, sometimes, you have to reach out to other people in the organization.

Sales Technique #43

Raise the Hard Issues Yourself

When I am trying to move closer to the top of that pyramid, trying to expand my relationship with a customer, I make a habit of identifying what I think the most difficult challenge in the relationship is going to be—and then bringing that problem up on my own, rather than waiting for the other person to do it.

You read right. What I do is try to put myself in the shoes of the other person, figure out what he or she would most likely object to in what I am proposing, and then talk about it first. A significant part of the art of selling is being more concerned about something than the prospect or customer is. This is exactly what you should do when you have a sales initiative that you feel could conceivably carry a problem for the person you are talking to. Your goals should be to say something along the following lines:

- "I'll tell you the truth. I am actually kind of concerned about the price. I am not sure it is right. What do you think?"
- "To be honest with you, I am a little concerned that the program might not be focused on the most important topics for your people. What do you think?"
- "Here is where it fits together, but I have to be honest with you, I am a little bit concerned about how the schedule could work. I do not know if it is going to work for your organization."
- "Here is the piece that we are not certain about. We are trying to find out whether or not this payment plan is right for your family. Help me out. What do you think are the pros and cons?"
- "Let me tell you what is keeping me up at night. I think I understand what you are trying to accomplish here, and I think we can do it within your timeline. But I am not entirely sure that it is something you feel comfortable trying to share internally with your people, and I want to be sure that I get it right—help me out."

Whatever it is we are trying to sell or sell more of—a piece of software, a series of training programs, whatever—we should identify a particular problem that could be waiting for us around the corner somewhere. We then try to raise that tough issue ourselves rather than wait for the customer to do so.

After all, what is the alternative? If we know we are going to get hammered on price but we do not have any meaningful feedback about what price the other person is looking for, why on earth would we wait for the person to give us an objection—or even worse, an objection that is not truly an objection that still stalls the sale completely?

When it comes right down to it, I would much rather understand the true dimensions of the problem that is keeping the other person from deciding to buy more from me. I would rather get that information straight than hear some vague brush off about needing more time to think about it or having to talk to somebody else.

By raising the most difficult issue ourselves, and not waiting for the prospect to either bring it up or, even worse, fail to bring it up, we get a much better sense of exactly where we stand when it comes to the initiative of getting this person to buy more from us.

Sales Technique #44

Develop Conversations, Not Lectures

I wish I could give you some spell that you could cast over your prospects that would instantly allow them to see the benefits of buying your product (or buying more of it), but no such spell exists. In the end, we will sell, or fail to sell, based on the quality of our conversations with our prospects and customers. Conversations are the foundation of selling. If we display genuine curiosity, and ask appropriate do-based questions, we will sell more of our products and services to our customers. If we don't, we won't.

What are do-based questions?

They are questions that focus, not on what we think the other person needs, or what we think his or her problem is, or what we think the potential pain is, but on what the other person is *actually doing*. If we focus only on what we consider the need, the pain, or the problem, then we won't get the whole picture of what's happening in the other person's world. We may get part of that picture, and we may close an initial sale, but to build a relationship for the future, we have to be willing to ask questions about what the other person does. For instance:

- "Hey, we've talked about your current salespeople—but how are you handling your training for your new hires right now?"
- "How long have you been trying to sell your motorcycle? What have you been doing to sell it so far?"
- "How did you handle this kind of staffing problem the last time around?"

All of these are do-based questions. And all of them are substantial improvements over silly questions like, "What would you change about your current so-and-so?" or "What don't you like about your present situation?"

Effective selling is an extended conversation that allows you to find out what the other person is doing and plans to do, review key objectives, and make those objectives your own.

If you never learn, or even bother to ask about, what this person is doing, or what this person's objectives are on the job or in other realms of his life, then you will not be in much of a position to initiate or expand the relationship.

Sales Technique #45

Don't Rush

No matter what you sell or where you sell it, your sale can typically be broken down into the following four stages: opening, interviewing, presenting, and closing.

Let's examine each stage individually.

- Opening. Also called prospecting, qualifying, or cold calling, this is where you contact someone you've never spoken to before (often by calling them on the phone) and determine whether there is a possible use for your product or service. You may set up an appointment or future call date at this stage.
- Interviewing. You learn the past, present, and future with regard to the prospect's use of your product or service. You find out what special problems have presented themselves recently. You learn other pertinent facts about the prospect.
- Presenting. You show exactly how your product or service can help solve the problems identified during the interview stage. You appeal to past successes with other customers.
- Closing. You ask for the sale.

It's possible that you can proceed through all four stages in a single telephone call. It's also possible that it will take you months or even years of appointments and follow-up appointments to go from making your cold call to reaching and completing the final stage. All that depends on the product or service you offer, your industry, its customers, the prevailing economic conditions—a number of different factors.

At any given point in the cycle, your objective is to move from where you are to the next stage. There is one rule, though, that you must bear in mind in considering the cycles I've outlined above. The rule is a simple one: the simplest and most reliable way to lose a sale is to move from one stage to the next before the prospect is ready to do so.

Many salespeople view their work as one gigantic closing stage. By failing to understand the cyclical nature of their work with a prospect, they rush things, and, accordingly, lose sales.

Let's say you have a garden. One morning you walk out into your garden and sow seeds for a tomato plant. If you're a smart gardener, you'll realize that it's going to take most of the summer for the tomato to make it from the seed stage into your salad bowl. If you wait a couple of weeks, see something vaguely tomato-like emerge from the ground, rip it up, and smother it with vinaigrette dressing, it's not going to make for a very good (or even edible) salad.

If, however, you give it time, let it mature, it will blossom into a juicy, ripe tomato. Then you can brag about it. But if you rush the process, you're not going to get anything for your efforts.

Selling is just the same. There are certain things for which you simply must wait. You should not attempt to walk into an office for the first time, shake hands with a prospect, and ask when the operations department would like to receive the first order. In this instance, you are attempting to rush from the interview stage into the closing stage, and your results will be disastrous. Most problems of rushing, however, are not that obvious. Perhaps you've talked a little bit about yourself, mentioned your product, admired the view, gotten a little past history, and received an assurance that what you're talking about "sounds interesting."

Are you ready to move on to the presentation stage? Maybe—and maybe not. The best option is usually to ask the prospect straight out: "Well, is there anything else you think I should know about your company, Mr. Smith?" Depending on the answer you get, you'll be able to gauge the prospect's enthusiasm for moving on to the next stage. When in doubt, err on the side of patience. There's no crime in saying, "Well, I've learned a lot about your company today; what I'd like to do now is set up an appointment for next week so I can go over a completed proposal with you."

Sales Technique #46

Always Try to Move the Sale to the Next Step

After I tell participants in my sales training seminars about the four stages of a sale, I ask them, "What's the objective of the first phase?" Inevitably people say things like:

- "The objective is to get the order."
- "The objective is to meet the person face to face."
- "The objective is to understand the customer."
- "The objective is to ask questions."
- "The objective is to close the sale."
- "The objective is to establish rapport."
- "The objective is to plant the seeds for a future relationship."

All of these answers are common. And all of them are wrong.

The objective of each phase in the model sales cycle is always to move ahead to the next phase. When you're opening, the objective is to get the prospect to agree to move forward into a meaningful interview phase. When prospects are in the interview phase, the objective is to get the prospect to help you track down the information necessary to develop a presentation that fits the prospect like a glove. When you're in the presentation phase, the objective is to conduct it so well that the prospect agrees to become a customer when you say, "It makes sense to me—what do you think?" (That question, of course, marks the fourth and final phase.)

Recently I was running a training program at a major investment house, a company that sells to people known as very high-net-worth individuals. I sat down with this person and we had an interesting discussion. He was saying to me how well he had done on this one particular high-net-worth individual. He had met with her once, and he thought the first meeting had gone quite well. I asked, "When are you going back to see the person?" because the strategy is to return to see the person. He said, "Steve, I've got that under control." I said,

"That's great! What are you going to do?" He said, "Well, I have to get information from her first, that is, I have to get her statements from her other investment house. And as soon as I get that, then I'm going to go back and make my appointment. So I feel pretty secure about that."

I said, "That's fine. Did you give her the special red envelope that you prepared especially for her so that she can send back the information that you need, or so you can pick it up when it's ready?" "Well, no, I haven't done that yet. I haven't even thought about that." I said, "Well, let me ask you a question. Did you talk to her assistant? After all, here's a person making, what, ten million dollars a year? She must rely pretty heavily on her assistant to keep track of everything. Did you mention to the assistant that you'll be back when the statements are in?" "Well, no. I didn't do that either." Then I asked, "When do monthly statements typically come in?" "Usually during the first week of the month." There was a long pause. This conversation was taking place on the twelfth of the month.

I said, "So what are you doing now?" He said, "I'm waiting for this person to call me. You know, it's a little late in the month, but she'll call. I'm sure she will. She told me she would call."

She didn't call. She never called. He never got that sale.

A prospect is somebody who is going to answer your questions. If you can't get a commitment for a specific next step of some kind, either on your part or theirs, then you're not dealing with a prospect.

So what strategy can you use to advance the sale? The first and most important one is always ask for the next appointment at the conclusion of a face-to-face meeting. No matter who you are, no matter where you are, no matter when you're seeing the person, ask for the next appointment. Now inevitably people say, "Well, Steve, it's a bad time to ask for an appointment. It's just before the holidays, just after the holidays, just before the summer, just after the summer, just before the winter, just after the winter." They give a million reasons why they can't ask for the next appointment. I can only tell you one reason why you should: to find whether or not the person is interested in working with you. If you run into someone for whom it's *always* a bad time, there's a problem somewhere.

Successful salespeople move the sales process forward, and they typically do this by closing each meeting with a request for a specific appointment for the *next* meeting. Some salespeople say, "Steve, how can I ask for an appointment? I've got no reason to come back yet!" Sure you do! Here's what top-performing sales reps say at the end of their appointments: "Mr. Prospect, I have an idea. What I'd like to do, instead of ending right now, is think about everything you've told me and look over all the notes I've taken today. And over the next week, I'm going to put together an outline of what we might be able to do for you, and I'd like to come back in a week and show you what our thinking is."

At that point you are in essence throwing the ball out to the contact. Your contact can either reach out and catch the ball, or he can deflect it, ignore it, and let it fall to the ground. In either case, *you'll know what's going on.*

Remember, the objective of the first step is to get to the next step, and that's all you want to do in each and every case. The only thing you should say to yourself when you evaluate your prospect is, "Have I advanced my sale?" If you have not, then you are not playing ball with your prospect, nor is your prospect playing ball with you.

Sales Technique #47
Sell Yourself on Yourself

Following are some ideas you can use to motivate yourself. Use them!

1. Don't Listen to the Radio During Your Morning Commute

Radio broadcasts are usually filled with lots of depressing news that you won't be able to do anything about anyway. You'll hear soon enough about any news of consequence; take the morning for yourself. Buy some motivational CDs or podcasts and make a habit of making the drive (or ride) in to work a time for positive messages and clear-headed, sober assessments of the day ahead. I know of one salesperson so committed to this principle that he honestly does not know whether or not his car radio even works!

2. Get Positive Reinforcement

I think it's fascinating how many successful sales "teams" there are—two individuals who sell completely independently, but who rely on each other for constant support, advice, and constructive criticism. For most of us, this really is a far better alternative than going it alone. If you can establish such a relationship in your current work environment, give it a try and see what happens.

3. Get Outside

Yes, you do need a lunch break. No, you shouldn't work through the noon hour. (My studies on this with salespeople lead me to believe that those who make a point of putting work aside for an hour and getting outside in the sunshine are actually more productive in terms of sales volume than those eager beavers who don't know when to quit.)

4. Leave Yourself Notes

"I can do it." "Most of the things I worry about never happen." "I have solved the problems of over 500 customers." Try to leave one on your desk Friday afternoon; you'll probably forget about it until Monday morning, when it will be a pleasant surprise.

5. Keep Things in Perspective

As I tell salespeople whom I'm training, "It's not brain surgery." It isn't! Missed calls, forgotten deadlines, problems with customers . . . challenging as they all can be, really aren't the end of the world. Sometimes things seem larger than they are. Try to keep that in mind as the day progresses.

Sales Technique #48

Know When to Retreat

Recently, I was in California working with a sales rep; we were talking about a prospect that he had been working on for the last four or five weeks. He'd gone to the prospect's office, gotten his information together, and made a good, solid proposal. In fact, his proposal was so good that I thought it really did make sense for us to do business with this company.

When I accompanied my rep on his third sales call to this company, I said to the prospect, "Bob, I really believe this proposal makes sense and we should go ahead." Bob was extremely interested in what we had to say, and he, too, felt it made sense. The only problem was that there were a couple of minor issues that still needed to be resolved; we would have to return with a more specific revised proposal.

Things looked good until my sales rep called again the following week and could not get Bob on the phone. After three attempts to get a return call, he called me up and said, "Steve, can you call Bob and see if you can get him on the phone?" I called once but didn't get him on the phone. Eventually, it became quite obvious that Bob did not want to return our calls. And the sale, for now, was dead.

Pretty common story, right? So what's the lesson to be learned? There are times when it makes sense to retreat and not waste any more of your time pursuing a prospect. Sometimes you're just not the right person to make the sale, and sometimes it's not going to happen, no matter how good you think you are and no matter how much sense it seems to make for you and the prospect to do business together. Sometimes you do the very best you can and it's pretty darned good, and things still don't work out.

Unfortunately, a lot of salespeople continue making calls well after this point of honorable retreat has passed. They continue going back to the same prospect on a regular basis.

I've talked to many salespeople who tell me that they make a hundred calls a day. In fact, what they do is call ten familiar people ten times a day. That may add up to a hundred *somethings,* but it's not a hundred calls in my book. I once ran into a sales rep who swore up and down that she had called someone 437 times in a vain attempt to get an appointment. I don't know whether or not I believe the part about the number of calls, but I do believe she never managed to schedule the appointment. The poor prospect must have dreaded the idea of developing a long-term business relationship with this person!

Some prospects will say "no" to you by never saying anything. You have to recognize when you're getting that message and be willing to move on. In the case of Bob, he'd really left us a message even though he hadn't left us a message. That is, his refusal to return the calls really was telling us something. He wasn't interested in doing business with us. So what's the point of going back and calling him over and over again?

In some cases, there really is nothing we can do to turn the situation around. Not many sales trainers will admit this openly, but in the real world, it's quite common to run into situations where your best and most appropriate response is to *leave the prospect alone and spend your time in a more efficient way* (i.e., call someone else).

Sometimes the chemistry simply doesn't click; sometimes you have no control whatsoever over the reason someone decides not to do business with you. Maybe you're too tall or too short or too redheaded or too something else that turns this person off. *Find someone else to talk to*—don't take it personally. You can't make a trusting business relationship happen by sheer force of will—it's a consensual dance between two people. If one doesn't feel right about the way something's going, there's no point in pressing the matter.

Time passes, things change. Don't be too concerned about temporary setbacks. Keep your eyes on your job, don't play head games, do your best, and you are, eventually, going to get business from a lot of the people who once didn't give you business. I promise. In the meantime, know when to back off.

There's a difference between being persistent and being obnoxiously persistent.

We will all lose battles. The objective is not to avoid losing a single battle, but to win the war. When it's time to retreat, pick up the phone and start prospecting so you can build a business relationship with someone new.

Sales Technique #49

Know When to Ask for Help

At a seminar not long ago, a woman came to me and she said that she was going to go to her manager and ask for some help in securing a sale. But she had misgivings. She said to me, "Doesn't it make me look weak if I can't close a sale by myself?" To which I replied, "No, absolutely not. In fact, if anything, it actually makes you look stronger."

Salespeople who know how to say, "Help me out here" to customers, prospects, or their own superiors are, in my experience, usually among the very top performers in their organizations. Let's look briefly at the different types of help you can get.

Appealing for help can mean simply *letting the customer correct you*. Superior salespeople know that when the customer corrects them, everyone wins. The best salespeople know how to elicit "corrections" that improve the relationship—and raise the quality of the information the salesperson gathers.

Let me give you an example. When I'm selling, I sit down and have an initial meeting with a prospect and then go through some of the basic steps of the sale. I'll explain a little bit about what I do and how I do it. I'll also find out what they do, how they do it, when they do it, where they do it, whom they're doing it with, and why they're doing it that way. But I *won't* try to close the sale at that point, nor will I follow up immediately with a formal outline. I'll find a way to get the customer to correct me.

I rarely come back with a formal proposal on the second meeting, and I may not even get to the formal proposal by the third meeting. Instead, I say to the prospect, "Let me think about what you and I have said. Let me put down some notes and what I will do is come back next week—say, Tuesday, at 10:00? Let me come back next week, and then I'll go through all the assumptions at that time."

What happens the following week? When I go through the various assumptions of the preliminary proposal, the prospect is either going to tell me that I'm right—or that I'm wrong. If I'm wrong, then by definition the prospect is offering meaningful feedback. He or she is telling me, "No, Steve. Here are the assumptions that you made that are wrong. And here are the correct assumptions." I know where I stand. I've been corrected. My formal proposal avoids some big problems.

At a presentation before the board of directors of a *Fortune* 500 corporation, my salespeople and I went through five assumptions that we had picked up from our initial conversation. Four of them were correct. The fifth, for some reason, we got wrong. Now I don't mean to say that it was totally wrong, and in thinking about it in retrospect, I realized that our contact might have actually given us some different information the first time than he did the second time. That's the way it works in sales—people get more direct with you as the relationship between the two companies becomes more important to them.

What mattered wasn't whether we were misled during our initial meeting, but the fact that, in the subsequent meeting, we worked toward a common goal of developing accurate assumptions in order to get the proper answer for this company. We got the help we needed from our prospect, and we ended up getting the sale.

You can also seek help from your managers and peers. I encourage salespeople to call and advise their supervisor as to the next step they're taking with a prospect after their initial meeting. If they need one of the other executives in the company to come along, that's an option too. But I recommend restricting this kind of help to second, third, or fourth meetings with key prospects. The first meeting really doesn't matter in sales, if you stop to think about it. Lots of people will agree to see you initially, but how many will commit to a date and time for that second meeting?

The odds are that you know people who know your product a lot better than you do. They're technical experts. Are you using those experts effectively to get additional information about your product to make a presentation? For example, are you saying to the prospect, "Here's an idea: let me bring back the technical expert next week. Instead of me simply coming back and explaining it, I'll let you talk to Tammi; she really is an expert in that particular area. I'd like her to meet you." That escalates the sale and gets more people involved in the process, which is usually a good sign. You may even be able to get *your* technical expert hooked up with the *prospect's* technical expert.

For crucial meetings with important prospects, it can often be a big help to get your sales manager—or, perhaps even more important, one of your company's technical people—to accompany you on a visit. So feel free to ask. That's what the superstars do!

Sales Technique #50

Follow Up the Next Day

Call or write your prospect the day after your visit. The vast majority of salespeople mean to do this but never get around to it. Build these contacts into your daily schedule or tickler system so you can be absolutely certain to follow up during that crucial period after the meeting.

Don't try to initiate contact any later than one day after the visit with the prospect. The whole point of this "supporting" maneuver is to re-establish your presence and your commitment to solving the prospect's problems. Do so tactfully and without being overbearing.

What might this sound like as a telephone call?

"Mr. Smith, this is Maude Powers at InfoWorld, Inc. I wanted to take a minute to thank you for taking time out of your schedule to meet with me yesterday. You know, I thought that meeting went really well. What did you think?"

Simple, and to the point.

I mention the phone contact first because that or e-mail seems to be the most likely means of communication for such a message in today's sales environment. I should point out, though, that an old-fashioned typed or printed letter on company stationery can win a good deal of positive attention. It's less likely to happen, of course, because time is at such a premium these days (and because so many salespeople honestly don't care to write letters). But that can work to your favor: your courteous, neat, well-written letter will stand alone. For instance:

Sept. 24, 2007

Dear Mr. Smith:

I wanted to drop a line to thank you for taking time out of your busy schedule to meet with me yesterday.

I found the ideas we exchanged very exciting, and I think you'll agree that there is the potential for a mutually beneficial relationship between your firm and ours. Mr. Smith, I hope you will feel free to call me if there are any questions or problems I can help you resolve.

Sincerely,

(written signature)

Maude Powers

PART IV

E-MAIL SELLING

E-mail selling is becoming more popular with the continued technological and communication revolution. But it's important to understand both its advantages and its limitations. There are a lot of things e-mail is great for—and some things you should never use it for. In this section, we'll talk about how to construct a clear, readable, useful e-mail and how to use it to supplement the other techniques you're using.

Sales Technique #51

Setting E-Mail Sales Goals

Here's what not to do. Don't spend all day writing e-mails designed to get you into more conference calls when you could be finding ways to get in front of more people face to face.

I wish I could tell you that the act of writing a better "let's have a conference call" e-mail message than your competition will, in and of itself, guarantee you a better relationship with, and better information from, your prospect.

But I can't.

If I were to tell you that, I would be engaging in wishful thinking, rather than strategic thinking. And wishful thinking, alas, is the one syndrome I have identified over the years that has inevitably led to failure among individual salespeople and organizations as a whole.

Here's what I can tell you. If you're smart, and if you implement the principles in this book, you can use e-mail more intelligently than your competition is currently using it, and thus get *more in-person meetings* and *accelerate your selling cycle.* In so doing, you will improve the quality of your relationship—and thus improve the quality of your information and your likelihood of closing the deal with people who keep moving forward through the sales process with you.

Ultimately, you should use e-mail as a tool to establish momentum with people who could conceivably buy from you. And I'm going to warn you ahead of time, if your job is to sell face to face, you're going to get the best results if you use e-mail to uncover reasons to get face to face with your prospects and customers.

Sales Technique #52

Craft the Perfect Message

There is no single perfect e-mail message that is applicable to all situations where we have the opportunity to move the sale cycle forward. There is, however, a set of standards we can apply to most of the e-mail messages that go out to prospects when we hit "send."

There are basically three questions that we have to answer. They are:

1. How long should the message be?
2. How detailed should the message be?
3. How casual should the message be?

Let us look at the first question: *How long should the message be?*
The best answer is: pretty darned short.

As a general rule, the *only* people I will read long e-mail messages from are people who are either my customers or people I am related to by blood. When it comes to anyone else, I either skip the message entirely or read the beginning and the ending and decide from there what I should do.

Be honest. This is probably very similar to your own standard. My guess is that, in your world, the only people whose long messages do get read are those from your own customers, your boss, or relatives.

We're creating messages that we want people to read. It is incumbent on us to keep our messages short if we want to get anything accomplished by means of an e-mail message that moves the sales process forward. How short? Again, think in terms of a single computer screen.

Everybody reads e-mail either by means of looking at a computer screen or by looking at a display that is considerably smaller, like a smart phone or a tablet. That means that we who write messages actually have a very small amount of space in which to make our point. For my money, it is best to keep the messages so short as to be impossible *not* to read if you glance at them.

I advocate an effective length of two to three sentences tops for the main portion of the message. Note that I am talking about the message that shows up in the body of the e-mail and not the subject line or the signature, which are separate animals.

How detailed should the message be? The message should go into relevant detail and feature few of those details. For instance, if the message can emphasize that we have worked with a company in this prospective customer's industry, that is the level of detail we want to encourage—but we do not want to spend more than a sentence or three exploring that. Be just as detailed as it takes to provoke curiosity and get a response—but no more detailed than that.

How casual should we be? The e-mail message has become, for so many of us, a replacement for verbal interaction. That means that during the course of our working day, if we are sending around e-mail messages internally, we may be tempted to adopt the same level of discourse that we would use if we were hanging around the water cooler. But in fact, if we are reaching out to a brand-new person or someone we have only recently spoken to on the phone, we actually have to assume a somewhat higher standard.

You never know. You might run into a grammar cop, someone who will disengage from your message the moment he or she finds a minor writing error in it. (This is another reason to keep the message short, by the way—fewer possibilities for error.)

Sales Technique #53

Break Up the Text

Here's a template for a basic format of an effective person-to-person e-mail message. This is a good model—but not the only possible model. It's a sound approach to a "basic" e-mail message that focuses on a Next Step.

Notice that its subject line connects to a date that coincides with the next step that we want to take in the sales relationship, and that the first line references a competitor or other company with which the recipient is familiar.

> Subject: Meeting on April 19
> MAXWIDGET
> We've done a lot of work for people in your industry, including MaxWidget. My boss suggested that you and I meet to discuss your widget retooling plans for the coming year.
> Could we meet this coming April 19 at 2:00 P.M. at your office?
> Sincerely,
> Mike Conway
> www.retooler.org
> 978-555-0555 (office)
> 978-555-5550 (cell)
> 978-555-5050 (home)
> CONFIRMING APRIL 19 MEETING AT 2:00 P.M.

There is absolutely no way anybody reading this message could misinterpret what it is about, get lost in a long paragraph, or misunderstand what kind of action is required or requested. Notice, too, that the message can be read in full on a single computer screen display.

The information at the beginning and end of the message is what is most important. If the reader is going to skip anything here, she is going to skip the material that shows up after the word *MaxWidget*.

The human mind is trained to ignore that which it does not process. By making an editorial decision to place the most important material at the beginning or end of the message, and by putting the least important information in the middle of the message, we are taking advantage of how the human mind works. All too often, people compose thoughtless e-mail messages where the most important information is buried in the middle of a long paragraph in a message like the following.

For instance, here's an e-mail that's guaranteed not to get attention:

Subject:　　　Your skyrocketing profits

Your profits certainly will start to skyrocket once you realize that we've worked with some of the key people in your industry, including MaxWidget. That's why my boss suggested that you and I get together. What would be a good time for us to hook up? Maybe sometime next week? Let me know.

Mike Conway

Sales Associate

Retooler

See the difference?

The first message is the message I strongly suggest you use as your model.

The second message is the message I want you to avoid like the plague. Dumb subject line. No Next Step request. Key information (the name of a competitor) buried in the middle of the text. No phone contact information. Nothing to catch the eye at the bottom of the screen. And even though it's quite short, it somehow seems long-winded.

Especially if you are at the beginning of the relationship and still trying to secure some kind of initial commitment; keep it short and make sure it follows the outline of the "good" template.

Sales Technique #54

Use the Subject Line

The subject line of the e-mail is the single most important determinant of whether the person will ever open, read, or acknowledge the body of the message—which means that we need to find a way to strategize that subject line at least as carefully and probably with much more thought than the body of the message.

Here are some examples of subject lines sent by real, live salespeople that are well intentioned enough and are certainly not making any attempt to mislead the reader but that still fail miserably at the task of getting the person to open the message and consider its contents.

Subject: Article

Is this a request that I send the person an article? Is this a request that the person be allowed to interview me for an article? Is this a request for an article that I have written? In fact, the salesperson wanted to send me an article. But if the point was to get me to open the message, the headline did a terrible job.

Subject: Your company's success

Again—there's nothing misleading about this. The salesperson really does want to talk to me about my company's success in the body of the e-mail. But what possible entry point to this subject does the single sentence here give me?

In fact, the person was trying to meet with me to discuss ways for me to expand my network of sales training franchises by means of display advertising. I'm not saying he necessarily had to put the words *display advertising* in the heading, but might it have made sense to connect the heading somehow to the goal I already knew about—namely, expanding my franchise network?

Subject: Tomorrow

This subject line is self-contained and has no meaningful connection whatsoever to the message it precedes. If I recognized whom the message is coming from, this could be a great heading because I would be interested in finding out what the person has to say about tomorrow. But in this case, I had no idea who this person was, and so I was left a message from a stranger about something unspecified that would happen tomorrow.

So much for well-meaning headlines that fail to engage the recipient. What do the best subject lines look like?

Here is one of my favorites:

Subject: June 23 meeting

The beauty of this heading is that it immediately answers the first question that everybody has when they are considering opening up an e-mail message, namely, "Is this something I really have to look at?"

In this case, the message makes it clear that it is something that requires attention, because there is a meeting in the short term. In fact, when I send this message, what I am doing is asking the person whether or not he or she is willing to meet with me on a certain date and time. I particularly like placing an emphasis on times and dates and months in headings, because it causes the recipient to wonder whether or not the message affects his or her immediate schedule, something that takes place during the next two weeks.

Commitments that take place within this particular time frame tend to mean much more than commitments that are made for three months or six months or nine months or twelve months away. The closer we get to that two-week time frame, the more meaningful that commitment is and the more important the communication about it becomes. So it stands to reason that a heading that focuses on a specific date within the next two weeks will probably have more interest than something that does not.

Here is another heading that works:

Subject: Joe Clark

This subject line is a good one to use when Joe Clark is someone
known to both the sender and the recipient of the message. If Joe
Clark is a personal acquaintance of the person I am trying to reach
out to, this is almost a guarantee that the recipient is going to open the
message and see what I have to say about Joe.

Subject: McClusky Industries

This is when McClusky Industries is either a competitor of the
e-mail recipient or a company otherwise familiar to the person I am
trying to contact. Ideally, it should be a company that I have worked
with, so I can build my message around the success I had in working
with McClusky in the past.

Sales Technique #55

Be Careful with Your Signature Line

Anyone who must make his or her way through a hundred or so e-mail messages sometimes notices the signature more readily than the body of the message. Why? Because human beings have a tendency to scan to the bottom of a message to see what the point of it is. We hit that page-down button or use our mouse to scroll to the very bottom of the message. What this means is that someone who receives a number of messages from us will, over time, receive more exposure to the signature we set up at the bottom of the message than to anything else we write!

It behooves us, then, to create a powerful and compelling signature, and to revise it from time to time so it retains the same basic theme but does not become so familiar that its message fades into oblivion.

Just as you would not send out a message to prospects or clients in written form that did not incorporate your company's logo and contact information on a sharp-looking piece of stationery, so you will also want to avoid sending out an e-mail message that contains no reference whatsoever to your company, its website, or your own role within the company.

Of course, there are some important differences between a carefully crafted e-mail signature and a good piece of stationery. For one thing, the stationery is a physical object, and it is an accepted convention to incorporate a logo at some point near its upper left-hand corner. There is no such convention these days regarding e-mail signatures, primarily because sending an image as part of a logo can set off spam filter alerts.

Here is a model signature to consider adapting:

Stephan Schiffman, President
D.E.I. Franchise Systems
www.dei-sales.com
"We Understand Sales"
123 Metropolitan Way
Metropolis, NY 10107
212-555-5555 (office)
212-555-5557 (cell)
212-555-5556 (home)

You read right—that's a home phone number. When I leave a positive impression with a prospect or customer, I want it to be reinforced with accurate information on how to reach me by phone at just about any hour of the night or day.

I do get a lot of resistance to this from salespeople, and I have told salespeople in training programs that it is a perfectly acceptable alternative to list one's cell phone number and main office number if these are the only two lines that you want to use for business purposes. But supplying the home number sends a message of accountability that is hard to forget.

If you remember anything at all about your e-mail message signatures, remember this: it should send the unspoken message that you wish to be accessible to the other person, and it should offer at least two valid phone options that the person can use to get in contact with you.

Sales Technique #56

Develop a Brand with E-Mail

We have entered a fascinating period in human history, one in which a single piece of information can emerge as a defining identifier and even a determinant of your own identity.

Think about it. If you have an e-mail address that connects to your business—*Johnsmith@ABCcorp.com*—then, when you share that information with someone, you are not merely giving them a way of getting in touch with you, but also sharing an important piece of who you are.

By giving the person that e-mail address, you give him or her the right to begin a correspondence with you, to maintain that correspondence over time, to forward it to other people, and to reach out to you at any and every time the person feels it's appropriate to do so—2:00 in the morning, 1:00 in the afternoon, whatever. In a strange way, your business persona *melds* with that e-mail address, in a way that your business identity does not meld with a phone number or a physical address. In cyberspace, your e-mail address is not only a way to get in touch with you, but an expression of your business self.

The reason I bring this up is to remind you that when you share your e-mail address with a business contact, you are basically sharing with them the right to archive and retrieve an ongoing series of messages that you share with them. Whereas we can throw away a written memo, it is quite common for electronic correspondence records to exist in three or four or more forms.

Just as your company goes out of its way to send specific brand messages about its products and services, you can and should use your e-mail address to evoke certain distinctive brand messages about you as a person: your trustworthiness, your ability to respond quickly to questions, your diligence in following through on commitments, and so forth.

Sales Technique #57
Start an E-Mail Newsletter

Just about everybody on earth likes to get something valuable for free. Someone may ask to receive something you or your business offer for free—an article or report, say. Signing prospects up for an e-mail newsletter is not spam, assuming that you give them the option to remove themselves from the distribution list, and assuming that you honor their request if they make it.

We must learn to operate between two all-too-familiar extremes—flooding somebody with irrelevant, unsolicited information on the one hand, and giving away too much free content online. Ultimately, of course, it's a matter of trial and error, but this is a balancing act that you and your company can, with just a little practice, get right.

People who agree to have their e-mail addresses added to a distribution list usually receive what is known as an "opt-in" newsletter. There's a pretty obvious reason for this name: they have opted in to the distribution list, meaning they have agreed to receive your newsletter.

The challenge, in working with this list, is to make absolutely certain that you are having a good dialogue with these people and that they feel the information they receive as a result of joining the list is worthwhile.

So what to send them? Well, approximately once a week, you can send an article. This will encourage a dialogue by means of passing along specific helpful information to this group. Some of those conversations turn into discussions about what you're selling. And some of those discussions actually turn into revenue for you and your company. The key to getting a good dialogue going is picking content that seems likely to be easy to implement for the people on your opt-in list.

One of the mistakes that people make about e-mail newsletters is that they make them too predictable. If the newsletter always comes out on Monday or always comes out on the first of the month, people become attuned to it—and that can be a bad thing. It's possible, of course, that the person is eagerly awaiting the latest installment of the e-newsletter, just waiting for the moment he or she can read the articles and forward them to everybody else in the organization. To my way of thinking, though, the odds are fairly long against that possibility. Much more likely is the scenario where the person gets habituated to seeing the newsletter show up in the mailbox on a certain day, and learns to ignore it.

So by altering the production schedule—by making it come out on the tenth day and then on the fourth day and then on the ninth day and then on the eleventh day—we help the audience develop a sense that the content is on the way at some point in the future. But we do not set up a pattern that they become so used to that they instantly delete the newsletter every Monday morning.

Along the same lines, I try to alter the headings I use in setting up the subject line for my e-mail newsletter. For example:

Subject: Stephan Schiffman on increasing the value of your key accounts

Subject: Ten "musts" for a successful speech

Subject: Sixty-second overview: Time management techniques for salespeople

Here's what I don't do for the subject line:

Subject: Stephan Schiffman's E-Newsletter, Volume 2, Issue 4

Vary your subject lines. Vary your content. And always highlight the benefit the person will receive by clicking on your message.

Sales Technique #58

Use E-Mails to Spread Information about Your Company

I love using e-mail to alert prospects and customers to the fact that an article about my company has shown up in a media source unconnected with my company. At the end of these messages, I usually suggest that the prospect and I get together to discuss new ideas. (But notice that the e-mail is technically "about" the link I'm passing along.)

Sometimes, when I suggest that salespeople use e-mail for just this purpose, they balk at the idea, and say:

"That's all very well for you, Steve—you're an author with lots of experience in getting articles placed. How the heck am I supposed to point people toward articles about my company when none exist?"

First of all, how sure are you that articles about you, your company, or your products really don't exist? Have you entered your own name or your company's name or the name of your most popular products and services into Google? Once you do this simple experiment—and we're talking about an experiment that takes only five to ten minutes to perform—my prediction is that you will find more than one article that's easy for you to pass along to prospects and customers by means of a message like the following.

Subject: Warranty coverage article you might find interesting
Hi Todd:

Below is a link for an article I came across in the Yahoo! News section the other day. It had some interesting points about our recent product launch, and I thought you might find particularly interesting the piece at the end about choosing the right warranty coverage.

http://linkarticle.com/87890708970

I have some ideas for Q4 I'd like to share with you over lunch next week. I'll call tomorrow to see when you're free.

Take care,

Susan

Even if you do have some coverage of your company, your products, or even yourself that you feel like sharing with the world of prospects and customers, it's likely that you could use more. Believe it or not, it's not at all difficult to put together a strong article that delivers value to your prospective customers; and it's only a very small investment of time, effort, cash, and energy to place those same articles in venues where they'll get more visibility than they're getting right now.

You can also make this sending-a-link message a "staying in touch" e-mail—one that doesn't (directly) reference a Next Step but simply gives you a reason to call the person a day or so after you hit "send." Here's how it works. First, you pick someone you want to reconnect with—say, that prospect who's been "pending" for the last three weeks and hasn't gotten back in touch with you about your proposal. Next, you select an article with diligent care, making sure that it really does match something that is happening in this person's world. Then, you place the easiest call in the world: "Hey, I sent you an article on yada yada yada; I don't know if you had the chance to see it, but I wanted to let you know that it's on your e-mail system. How are things?"

Sales Technique #59
Build Your Website

Suggesting that the person visit your website and then get back to you to let you know what he or she thinks of it is not a great strategy for moving the sales process forward.

I get this all the time, usually from people I don't know who phone me and e-mail me and who are trying to establish some kind of first contact. "Hey, let me give you my website address. I want to know what you think of it."

This is basically the same as requesting that the person read your brochure and then give you a call to let you know his or her thoughts about it. If you can beat your quota by doing that, my hat is off to you, but I suspect that neither you nor any other salesperson on earth can pull off that trick.

We want so desperately to think that we are satisfying the other person that we sometimes fall back into the habit of not challenging the prospect in any way. "Oh, I'm not asking you to actually *do* anything meaningful in this relationship—just, in your off hours, of which I know you must have plenty, to review my brochure—er, website—and tell me what you think of it."

This loses sight of the fact that there *has to be some kind of creative tension in any selling relationship.* If the prospect is already happy doing exactly what he or she is doing right now, that person would have no need to talk to a salesperson. (Remember: your chief competitor is the status quo.) We, as salespeople, have to challenge our prospects' conception of what they are doing right now; we have to learn what they're doing right now and shake things up a little bit. We think it is possible that there may be a match between what we do and what they do. We think that the match may have aspects of value that they have not previously considered.

You don't want to overwhelm the person. At the same time, you don't want to fall into the trap of avoiding any possible tension in the exchange.

Ask *directly* for a *meaningful* Next Step. Instead of saying or writing, "Why don't you take a look at our website and then e-mail me back," call and say this, either directly or by means of a voice mail message:

"I came across an article that I want to e-mail you; it is a link that shows up on our website and it is a little hard to find. I am going to send you the link because I think it has some good ideas for your blah blah blah initiative, and then I will call you tomorrow. I have some thoughts on how it might affect your business. I am planning on calling around eight. Talk to you then!"

Then send the article—as a link, not as an attachment. And call when you said you were going to call.

I've trained salespeople on this stuff for over a quarter of a century. So you can imagine how it makes me feel when I get a prospecting call and I hear a salesperson say, "Hey, that's okay. Do me a favor. Jot down the name of my website and take a look at it. Then let me know what you want to do."

I hang up instantly. This is the sort of thing that might make it sound as though some kind of meaningful discussion has taken place. But in fact, there is no discussion at all.

How likely would you be to invest a chunk of your day reviewing the contents of a website based on a thirty-second discussion with a total stranger? Not very likely at all. So, if you are going to close the call with something, close it with an attempt to meet again or talk again or a suggestion about a way that you might be able to get face to face with the person at some public event. Do not issue meaningless and irrelevant suggestions that the person monitor your website. It is just not going to happen.

Sales Technique #60

Start a Blog

Most people who write blogs write them for very small audiences. That's the bad news about blogging. What is the good news about blogging? The good news is it is, technically, free. Or at least part of the monthly package you are paying for anyway to connect to the Internet.

The six-million-dollar question is this: why should anyone be interested in reading your blog? Well, there are two possible reasons for people to be interested. Either what you write will entertain them, or what you write will be useful to them.

Let's tackle entertainment first. Many, many people spend large amounts of time, effort, and energy trying to be controversial, funny, or otherwise engaging by means of a blog, and very few of them succeed. Of those who do succeed, only a tiny minority attracts any audience of any size. The question here is not whether you are capable of writing something that makes *you* feel good for having written it, but whether you can write something that will enhance the visibility—and perhaps even the profitability—of your products and services. So I am going to suggest that you focus, not on tickling people's funny bones—or, God forbid, infuriating people by being purposely controversial or abusive—but rather on being useful. The job of your blog should be to keep people abreast of new developments that they are likely to be interested in, given their status as your customers or prospects.

Think of your blog as something that people familiar with your stuff, or searching for something like it on the Internet, will be happy to stumble across. Use your blog to:

- Tell people about changes in your product or service lines
- Tell people about changes to your website
- Share free advice that people can use instantly on how to do what they do better

- Share links to articles of interest to people who fall into your market niche
- Collect responses and feedback from blog readers
- Update your readers about a business or news event that connects to their business objectives

Of course, each of these ideas is something you could also adapt to your e-mail newsletter copy.

Two of the most popular sites through which to set up a blog are Blogger.com and LiveJournal.com. Check them both out.

If you want, and if the editors of the group agree, you can include your name and contact information in the signature of your posting software and share an occasional article or resource or comment. As I say, though, you shouldn't expect this to turn into a revenue source.

Sales Technique #61
E-Mail Selling to Executives

Suppose you follow the advice of the various "take it to the top" C-level selling experts, muster your courage, and actually make that dreaded call to Jane Intimidator, the CEO of Amalgamated Data.

Please understand: At this stage I am not talking about sending a "blind" e-mail message to Jane. I am talking about calling her up on the phone and asking her for a meeting.

And suppose that Jane is actually willing to meet with you. Suppose that she actually remembers and is present for your meeting when you show up at her doorstep.

How long do you think that discussion with Jane is actually going to last?

If Jane is like most of the CEOs that I deal with, it's going to be a pretty brief conversation. Jane got to be CEO of Amalgamated Data by delegating work to other people. So whatever it is I am trying to sell Jane, you can bet that she is not going to sweat out the details of the decision to implement it. Even if she likes my suggestion (and eventually signs on), somebody else is going to do the heavy lifting.

No, the best outcome I can hope for in that situation, and in any similar situation with a similarly high-powered executive, is to receive an endorsement from Jane that allows me, not just to *talk* with Joe Achiever, the high-flying VP of operations for Amalgamated Data, but to do so *under the auspices* of the CEO, Jane Intimidator.

Before I leave my meeting with Jane, I want to ensure that I can keep her in the loop—and broadcast the message to others at Amalgamated Data that Jane is engaged with me and supports my efforts. I want Jane to be kept up to date on exactly what happens between me and Joe, and I want that to happen in a way Joe has to respect.

It might be nice if Jane would agree to meet with me again so I can update her on exactly what is happening between me and Joe. But in the real world, this is not very likely.

No, what is actually likely to happen is that Jane will agree, if I ask her directly, to let me update her on all the important conclusions that Joe and I reach *after* Jane refers me to him.

How do I want to make those updates to Jane? Well, if I know how Jane likes to communicate, I am going to pick the medium she is most likely to engage with, review regularly, and trust. But in a lot of these situations, I really will have no idea what Jane's preferred method of communication is going to be, so I am going to suggest, by default, that I keep Jane—and everybody else I connect with at Amalgamated Data—up to date by means of e-mail. That's why I'm going to ask Jane to give me her e-mail address so I can personally give her a summary, from time to time (not every day), of exactly what I am doing with Joe. And so I can copy Joe on the very same message.

It is very important to understand that when I ask Jane for her e-mail address so I can give her *occasional* updates, what I am really doing is setting up a barometer of sorts that will tell me about the quality of my communication with Jane. I want to gauge Jane's willingness to get an occasional summary of how my initiative is going, and the prospects that it really will add value to her organization.

If Jane tells me, "No, I don't want to give you my e-mail address; I get enough messages already . . . work with purchasing," that is really not a good sign that I should invest a lot of time and effort and energy in my discussions at Amalgamated. It is possible, of course, that Jane would rather hear about how my discussions with Joe are going by some other medium, but if the simple request for an e-mail address falls flat, then I know that there is likely to be a problem somewhere down the line.

My experience is that CEOs tend to be very direct about things like this. If they are asked a direct question, they will give you, more often than not, a direct answer. That really is the key: You have to be willing to ask them a direct question. You have to learn not to beat around the bush.

Another big issue in this situation is trust. We have to make it absolutely clear to Jane that we will not be bombarding her with fifty e-mails a day. Who could blame her for wanting to avoid that?

In this case, when you are dealing with a very high-level person, you may not be able to secure a Next Step that takes the form of a face-to-face meeting with the very topmost person in the organization. (No matter what anybody says, it is unlikely that you will be able to work directly with the CEO of a large organization, and it is unlikely that he or she will agree to meet with you again one on one.)

The whole point of the meeting, from the CEO's point of view, will simply be to plug you in with the right people in the organization. That's if you're lucky. That's the best possible outcome to that meeting. In that case, you will want to "take the temperature" of the relationship and just make sure that the CEO really does want results of the kind you think you can deliver. If so, he or she should have no problem agreeing to a *brief* e-mail message from you that summarizes how the initiative is going.

Once you establish that, the e-mail message you prepare for the CEO will have the most remarkable effect on others in the organization. It will remind Joe Achiever that you are in fact working with Jane Intimidator's blessing. During your next discussion with Joe, you can make it clear that you set up this arrangement with Jane, that she has given you her e-mail address, and that she wants to have a concise summary of exactly what you found out between now and the middle of March.

Sales Technique #62
Five E-Mail Mistakes

Mistake #1: Not Asking for, or Confirming, or Setting a Next Step

Not building a reference to some kind of Next Step into your e-mail, or preparing for one you plan to ask for, means breaking a basic commandment of selling.

You are a salesperson. Your income is built on asking for, and receiving, Next Steps. You are communicating by e-mail with someone to whom you wish to sell. It follows that your every communication should either propose, or directly or indirectly reference, what's happening next, or could happen next in the relationship.

Use a personalized e-mail message to:

- Request a face-to-face meeting at a specific date and time
- Confirm a face-to-face meeting at a specific date and time
- Send along a link to an article of interest, then phone the person afterward to make sure the person saw the link
- Say that you have a new idea to discuss and suggest a specific date and time for doing so (This is often helpful after a presentation has gone poorly.)
- Set expectations for an upcoming meeting at a specific date and time
- Establish timelines with a current customer
- Float an idea for a proposal before you actually deliver the formal proposal at a specific date and time.
- Pave the way for a phone call at a specific date and time that will set up a face-to-face meeting
- Confirm the date and time of a postmeeting "debriefing" appointment before you deliver a presentation to a committee or meet with a group

Mistake #2: Tone Mismatch

I'm assuming you were careful enough to send an *initial* message that struck a professional tone and piqued the other person's interest. What I'm talking about here is the message you send *in response to an incoming message from the other person.* Often, the messages salespeople send out in such situations are hastily composed, and they miss out on important conversational cues from the other side.

Suppose you get the following message:

To: Jerry Salesperson
From: Mark Bigshot
Subject: Re: Beating Quota By 15 Percent in All Seventeen of Your
            Territories

Hello there, Jerry:
This does sound intriguing. Alas, I'm not available to meet with you on April 12.
Is there any time the following week that we could get together? I am free from 2:00 P.M. to 3:00 P.M., Monday through Thursday. What's the best day for you?
Best,
Mark

What can you conclude about the person's communication style, just from those few sentences? Well, for one thing, this is someone who takes a good deal of time to compose text with care. All the capitalization is correct. All the punctuation is correct. All the sentences are complete. Mark even used the word *Alas*, which is at least circumstantial evidence of an English major somewhere in his family tree.

Since you know that you're dealing with a careful writer who adopts a studious, careful, almost academic tone, you should do your best to mirror that tone in the message you send back.

Even though you'll have to take a few extra minutes to compose a sentence or two that matches Mark's studious tone, that's the right way to go. For instance:

To:	Mark Bigshot
From:	Jerry Salesperson
Subject: Re:	Beating quota by 15 percent in all seventeen of your territories

And hello to you, Mark:
Thanks so much for getting back to me so quickly.
Could we possibly meet in your offices on Monday, the 19th of April, at 1:30 P.M.? I have a meeting that morning at Centennial Bank.
Looking forward to hearing from you,
Jerry

Unless you are absolutely certain you have achieved what might be called a "verbal" level of e-mail interaction with your correspondent—the kind of relationship in which an occasional misspelled word or forgotten punctuation mark will do you no discredit—you should go to the trouble of composing your message carefully, checking it for grammar and spelling errors, and perhaps even asking somebody else to review it before you send it out. Hitting send before you are really ready to is one of the most common causes of "e-mail stress" among salespeople.

Mistake #3: Sending Attachments Too Early in the Relationship

Sometimes, spam filters will refuse a message that carries an attachment, or will regard an image within the message as an attachment. Even if the message with an attachment or image makes it through, people will generally shy away from a message from an unfamiliar correspondent that has an attachment. Can we blame them? This is how computer viruses are spread. Leave off the attachment until the other person tells you that it is okay to send one.

Mistake #4: One-Word Messages

Even in response to a one-word message from the other person. Even if the person does understand you (which is far from a certain thing), you will run the risk of being perceived as arrogant. Do something a little more creative than writing the words "yes" or "no" in the body of the message.

Mistake #5: Being (Perceived as) a Jerk

Here's the interesting thing about e-mail: it is extremely easy to misinterpret.

We, as readers of e-mail, lack any meaningful visual information from the sender. (We can't read body language or facial expressions, the way we would in a real-life, one-on-one conversation.) Similarly, we as readers lack any information about the pitch or tone of the sender's intended "voice." (We can't hear whether the other person intends a remark to sound facetious, for instance.)

But, to the writer, e-mail correspondence often feels very much like verbal communication—so much so that many people who "let it all hang out" while writing messages type out things that look strange, offensive, or even menacing in an e-mail message . . . but wouldn't draw a moment's notice if the same words were spoken casually.

Don't let the other person conclude that you are a jerk. In the world of e-mail, all it really takes to "be" a jerk is for you to inadvertently give someone the ammunition necessary to conclude that you are one. Stay away from sarcasm and irony; make sure nothing you've written could possibly be misconstrued.

PART V

CLOSING THE DEAL

All sales, as you've learned in this book, have four parts: opening, interview, presentation, and closing. For some reason, closing is one that a lot of salespeople struggle with. I've dealt with this in detail in *Closing Techniques (That Really Work!)*. Here we'll learn the basics of how to successfully get to an agreement and what a well-concluded sale looks like.

Sales Technique #63

Ask for the Sale

Part of my preparation when I get a contract to train salespeople at a large corporation is to accompany a few of the company's reps on calls. I speak to the sales managers and corporate executives, of course, but it is going "on rounds" with the sales reps that provides me with the best picture of the company, its product, and the way it is sold. As a result, I'm better able to tailor the class to the students' needs.

But one thing I observe regularly—or at least more regularly than I'd like—is reluctance on the part of salespeople to ask for the sale. Often they'll say something like, "Suppose I call next Tuesday to get your decision." Or "Do you know when you'll make a decision?"

I suspect there are a number of reasons reps don't ask for the sale. Some may be too polite. They feel that asking just then, face-to-face, might put the prospect on the spot, perhaps embarrassing him or her. Or at least I think that's what most of them tell themselves.

But I believe the main culprit is a lack of confidence in their presentations. They don't believe they've earned the sale and want to put off what they assume (usually correctly) will be a "no."

The bottom line here is *that you have to ask for the sale no matter how badly you think the presentation went.*

Why? For one thing, if the answer you receive is "no," what difference does it make if you find out now or two weeks from now? In fact, finding out that the answer is negative now is probably better for you in the long run; it will keep you from worrying about and dwelling on this sale and force you to concentrate on another prospect.

More important, if you get a "no" now, you may be able to find out what went wrong and correct your presentation—*before* a final decision is made—and salvage the business. I make a special point to ask for the sale if I sense something is amiss. Then, if I'm told I didn't make the cut, I say something like: "You know, Bill, I was certain I was on track here. Can you tell me where I went wrong?"

Sometimes I get an answer like, "We just got a new budget and can no longer make as large a commitment to training as we'd anticipated." But often I'll be told a specific area where my proposal went awry. That gives me an opening to try again, to say, "Gee, I should have thought of that myself. Can I rework this and come back to you with a new proposal?"

Getting a "no" gives me an opportunity I never would have had if I waited. Waiting typically means getting a response after a decision is made, when it's too late to do anything but turn tail and walk away with as much grace as you can muster.

But there's another issue here apart from how well the presentation went. Not asking for the sale makes you seem less confident in your ability to make the prospect company perform more efficiently, earn more money, and/or put out a better product.

If you lack confidence, you become tentative—and you make it easy for prospects to say "no" to you. Swagger alone won't necessarily clinch a sale. But a sales rep who demonstrates confidence inspires confidence.

If you're not convinced that your product or service is just what the prospect needs, it's possible that you haven't done your homework. You haven't spoken to enough people in the company to discover a way to make your product a meaningful part of the prospect company's process. That falls on you. The main focus of the sales product is for you to find a way to make your product seem invaluable to the prospect.

But there's another possible scenario. Perhaps you lack confidence because your product really *is* inferior to others on the market. That happened to me on one of my earliest jobs. I was a good, aggressive salesman, and at first I was able to make a decent enough living, at least for a single young man—even one who lived in Manhattan. But it got to me after a while.

Often the sales I made were because my company was willing to cut prices to the bone, not because the product was the best choice available. Proof of that is that there were very few repeat orders.

I quit after only about six months, determined never to put myself in that kind of situation again. I was young, carefree, and a little idealistic. I know we don't all have those choices. But this is something we should strive for.

Sales Technique #64

An Objection Is an Opportunity

Sometimes, of course, you'll encounter obstacles during your presentations. Typically, salespeople refer to these obstacles as "objections."

I really don't like the term "objections." It's better to think of them as responses. When someone tells you there's a problem with what you've proposed, that shows that the person is actually listening and thinking about your products and services. That means you have the opportunity to advance the sale by asking questions, by getting "righted," and then putting the spotlight on your organization's relevant resources.

By raising an issue—rather than flatly rejecting and refusing to discuss your recommendation—your contact is trying to draw your attention to something. Try to ask questions that will help you get to the bottom of whatever it is that the prospect is trying to get you to notice. Remember: any feedback from the prospect is a form of "getting righted!"

As salespeople, we have to be extremely careful about the assumptions we make when we encounter obstacles late in the sales process. Very often, we hear a negative response and assume that it is an objection, especially when it concerns price. Sometimes what sounds like an "objection" about your payment terms is really a question about how much flexibility you're willing to show in invoicing. Sometimes what sounds like rock-hard price concerns mask other issues, such as a need to be persuaded about your commitment to follow through and a desire to make sure that what you sell actually delivers the benefit you promise.

Price "objections" in particular should not be taken at face value. Let me give you an example. Think about a time you bought an appliance, like a stereo or a television. What happened? Perhaps you walked into the store having decided that you wouldn't spend more than, say, $500. Perhaps you gave the store attendant a particular price range when asked about price, and perhaps he or she walked you over to a certain model.

What happened next? You probably found yourself bombarded with reasons why that particular model was just perfect for you. All the person has asked is how much you want to spend, and suddenly you've got this cascade of features coming at you, all apparently based on that one single piece of information: the price. Whatever intelligent interaction there was between you and the salesperson has stopped cold. If you're like me, you're quickly looking for reasons to avoid making a purchase commitment at this point.

Now think about what happens when you run into an intelligent salesperson in a retail setting, someone who's willing to ask you just a few questions about what you're doing, why you're doing it that way, and what you hope to do in the future. This kind of salesperson can often change your "I'm only spending $500" mindset into a "$750 seems worth it" mindset in a matter of minutes, and with very little effort.

When we hear what we think is a price objection we should get to the bottom of the issue by asking intelligent questions before we commit to solving any problem the prospect raises.

Here are three simple steps for handling responses effectively:

1. Identify/isolate the issues. Ask questions like, "What makes you say that?" or "Why that amount?" or "How does this concern fit into your goal of . . . ?" Then ask yourself: Do I really understand the problems my prospects typically face? What is this problem, really? (Never forget: your prospect's initial assessment of an issue may be masking a deeper challenge.) Exactly how is this particular issue affecting this particular prospect, right now?

2. Validate the issue. Figure out what its real-world dimensions are. Talk the challenge through openly and honestly with your prospect. (For instance: "You're not alone. My experience is that, if people have a problem with our delivery dates, it usually comes up at this point in the discussion. Let's see what we can

do.") Don't run away from the problem or pretend it doesn't exist. Offer appropriate additional information and help your prospect reach a logical conclusion.

3. Resolve the issue. This may be easier to do than you think. While every prospect is unique, accomplished salespeople tend to face the same half-dozen or so challenges over and over again within any given target industry. Don't use a cookie-cutter approach, but do share appropriate anecdotes and bring your personal and organizational experience to bear in developing a creative solution.

Sales Technique #65

Overcome the Money Objection

Recently, at a meeting with the top brass at a large bank, I was following my own advice and encouraging my prospects (in this case, it was a committee) to help me compose the proposal I would eventually present.

When it came to money I started getting funny signals. I'd talked about the plan I wanted to develop for the bank, I'd tried to identify the major objectives of the people I was working with, and I'd stated a rough (read: negotiable) dollar amount that was appropriate for the work I anticipated doing. I said, "Let me give you a feeling for what I think this is going to cost." I named a figure. The president of the bank looked at me, smiled, and told me he had no problem with the amount of money I had mentioned. But the chief executive officer saw things differently.

He said to me, "I'm not sure that I want to pay that kind of money."

Because I'd been attentive during the interviewing stage, I knew that the company, although large and profitable, was growing fast, and was experiencing the kinds of cash constraints common in a high-growth environment. Companies that are growing rapidly tend to eat up a lot of cash. So instead of perceiving the chief executive officer's comment as a challenge to my program's viability, or as the first salvo in a negotiating war over my fees, I reacted to it as though it were an expression of a concern about cash flow.

Which, it turned out, is exactly what it was.

I offered the chief executive officer the opportunity to pay off my fee over an extended period, and he smiled broadly and said he thought that could work. A week later I made my presentation, asked the principals what they thought about what I had to offer, and closed the sale.

If you truly listen to your client, if you avoid the temptation to assume that this prospect's price objection is the same as the last person's price objection, you'll be in a much better position to get the information you need to put together a presentation that closes.

After all, can you imagine what would have happened in that case if I'd assumed that their financial situation was exactly like that of the last prospect I'd met with? If I'd held off discussing the issue of price until the very end of the process? I would have named a figure. The president would have said it made sense. The chief executive officer would have had his reservations. Everybody would have said that the committee needed time to think. I would have left. At some point the chief executive officer would have pointed to his (valid!) cash flow concerns, and someone could have pointed out, rightly, that I had not mentioned anything about any payment plans. The committee would have had to assume that I would require a standard half on signing, half on completion, and could have felt uncomfortable asking me for other terms—if they'd thought about asking at all. And I would have lost the sale!

Sales Technique #66

Overcome "I'll Have to Think about It"

If you hear "I'll have to think about it," or some variation on it, after you've made your presentation, say something like this:

You: Well, Mr. Prospect, you know, as I finished this, I have to admit, I was a little concerned that I might have put too much emphasis on the (and here pick some nonthreatening aspect of your presentation). What did you think?

What you've done here is you've given the prospect the option to disagree with you. You've deliberately picked a relatively innocuous element of your sales presentation, and you've said to the prospect, "Hey, I made a mistake here, didn't I? Please correct me."

Nine times out of ten, if you've done your preparatory work correctly, and if you say something like the above, expressing your own concern that you may have put too much emphasis on the question of how to train the prospect's people to use your widgets, you'll hear something like this in response:

Prospect: No, actually, it's not the training I'm concerned about. We've just got a problem with your specs. I don't think the people out in Dubuque are going to be able to fit this into their production patterns.

You've uncovered the real obstacle! And from here you can work with the prospect to fine-tune what you have to offer.

I'm very big on success stories. Stories are very powerful sales tools. If you can highlight an encounter with a particular customer of yours who did overcome the same or a similar obstacle, do so. If you don't know enough about your customers to be able to do this comfortably, find out!

If you encounter resistance along the lines of "I'll have to think about it" after you've made your formal presentation, isolate a part of the presentation, express your concern to the prospect that you may have mishandled it, and ask for help. In the vast majority of cases, the prospect will reassure you that what you've identified is not in fact the problem, and will say something like, "What we're really still thinking about is . . ."

As common as "I'll have to think about it" can be, and as frustrating as "I'll have to think about it" can be, it's really not the worst thing that can happen to you at this stage. You want to keep things moving ahead smoothly, and you certainly don't want to run the risk of polarizing the good working relationship you've worked so very hard to develop with your prospect.

Sales Technique #67

Deal with an Outright "No"

"It's just not right for us."

"I think we'll pass."

"Thanks, but no thanks."

Assuming you have followed my advice about developing your formal sales proposal in concert with the prospect, you should use the full-fledged "Mr.-Prospect-I'm-genuinely-surprised-please-tell-me-what-went-wrong" technique only when you receive an outright "No."

This will be quite rare, but you should be prepared for it. The best approach to an outright, no-daylight rejection following your proposal is simple: take responsibility. Find out what you did wrong. After all, if your prospect, after working with you to isolate all the issues and objectives, after telling you everything about his or her objectives in a given area, and after having told you to your face that it was likely that you'd close the sale if you hit all the points the two of you identified together—if, after all that, the prospect can turn around and give you a flat "no," then you've got a right to be surprised. You've got a right to ask where things went off the rails.

The "taking responsibility" approach is predicated on your well-placed, unshakable confidence in your product or service. You are not supposed to be angry at the prospect, but expressing your (no doubt genuine) surprise. The aim of the technique is exactly what you tell the prospect your aim is: to find out where things went wrong so you can work from there!

Sales Technique #68

Keep the Closing Positive

Some salespeople have come up to me during breaks in my seminars and told me that they're uncomfortable with many of the "closing tricks" they've read about in sales books.

My comment to them is that they *should* be uncomfortable with those tricks. They're manipulative, unprofessional, and ineffective.

If you've spent most of your time gathering information, your plan will actually make sense to the prospect. That means you won't need fancy closing tricks. Instead, you can simply say: "It makes sense to me—what do you think?"

This is the world's simplest—and most effective closing technique. This strategy assumes that you have spent most of your time gathering and verifying information about what the prospect is doing and how you can help him or her do that better.

When we use this "makes sense to me" closing strategy I've just described, we're forcing the other person to react. It's a little bit like tossing a ball out to the prospect: he or she has to respond somehow. If the person catches the ball and tosses it back to us by saying, "Yes, it does make sense; when can we start?" then we know we've closed the sale. By the same token, the other person could respond, "No, it doesn't make sense." Then we can ask, "Really? Why not?" At that point, more often than not, we're going to learn exactly what is standing in the way of our doing business together.

And that's the key point to remember. When people tell us why our suggested proposal *doesn't* make sense, they are actually telling us what is wrong and how to correct it. The relationship is still moving forward. We've been "righted."

Sales Technique #69

Know When to Stop Talking

Years ago, I saw a poster in my insurance agent's office that I found
extremely crude—at first. It said:

> *SET IT UP*
> - Set it up
> - Put it down
> - And shut up

But the more I thought about it days later, the more I came to
recognize the wisdom of those words, especially when it comes to sales.
It's impossible to quantify, but I'm convinced that a decent percentage
of sales are lost because reps just don't know when to quit talking.

Basically, there are two schools of sales protocol. One says that sales
are made and lost in the presentation—that is in the words brought to
the table by the sales rep. The other believes the sales rep's job is not to
talk but to listen to what the prospect has to say.

As is always the case, the answer lies somewhere in between. Clearly
the sales rep needs to speak, and just as obviously the sales rep needs to
listen. But that doesn't always happen in the right proportions.

Most often than not, the problem is associated with the sales rep's
ego. We've all met the rep who thinks he knows it all—and isn't shy
about informing everyone around him about how smart he is. Let's
assume for a minute that you are an expert in your product. You know
how it is manufactured. You know how it can be used. You know how
it should be sold.

What happens if someone comes in and tells you everything you
know is completely false, that he knows the real truth and you ought
to be grateful that he is willing to share it with you? What do you
think you'd tell him? Do the words "shut up" come to mind?

Let's say someone comes in and spends the preponderance of time
at the meeting talking about her exploits—how many widgets she's

sold, how many companies she works with, all the places her widgets are used—without a word about how you might use them. What might your reaction be? Do the words "shut up" come to mind?

Or how about a sales rep who does ask appropriate questions but doesn't bother to listen to your answers. As a result, his proposal is wildly off base. What might your reaction be? Do the words "shut up" come to mind?

I have a simple know-when-to-stop-talking plan. Before I go into a meeting I note what I want to accomplish. It may be just to get some questions answered. It may be to see if I can get an okay to meet additional folks at the company. It may be to get "righted"—that is to see if the information I've received to date—and my interpretation of it—is accurate. Once I achieve my goal (and set up the next step), I get out of there as quickly as I can politely do so.

The shut up rule is even more important when you present. You offer your proposal, repeat points of emphasis, and then keep quiet. You might ask if there are any questions, any points that need clarification, or even ask for an order.

But don't keep repeating yourself. Very few things are worse than a salesperson droning on and on, repeating points as though the prospects were idiots and didn't get the point the first four times he brought them up.

The bottom line is if your message is appropriate and properly delivered, the prospect will get it. If it's not, then no matter how much you talk you won't be able to overcome that blunder.

Sales Technique #70
Be a Leader

Throughout the interviewing stage, and certainly before you reach the point at which you're ready to make a presentation to your prospect, you should solidify your image as a leader.

For many salespeople, this seems to get a little tricky, because your aim in the early part of the sales process is to get the prospect to talk to you about objectives and what they do. How, you may be asking yourself now, are you supposed to do that and get the prospect to see you as a leader?

Actually, there's no contradiction at all. Think back to the advice I gave you about handling the interviewing stage. I said that you should convey the message that it's good business to do business with you, and then steer the conversation in such a way that the prospect does the talking.

Yes, I said, "steering." Steering a car means driving the car! Steering your conversation with the prospect means driving that conversation!

We often get hung up on definitions. Sometimes when we hear the word "leadership," we automatically think of people telling other people what to do. A real leader knows that if that's all you focus on, you're dead.

A leader inspires.

A leader knows what he or she knows.

A leader does not try to hide what he or she doesn't know.

A leader knows how to get the best out of the people with whom he or she works.

A leader adds value to just about everything he or she touches.

A leader makes people feel more important after meeting with them.

A leader points the way after studying all the angles.

A leader is accountable.

A leader takes the good with the bad with equanimity.

A leader keeps an open mind.

A leader sees opportunity even in a setback.

A leader seizes opportunity.

A leader knows when to trust instincts and when to ask for further information.

A leader isn't afraid of new ideas.

A leader knows that if good business relationships come first, money usually follows.

A leader knows that open dialogue is essential to true creativity.

A leader thinks in the long term.

A leader knows there is no point in burning bridges.

A leader doesn't have to cajole others into being truthful; they do it of their own accord.

A leader takes a relatively long time to make a decision—and will generally stick with that decision, even in the face of obstacles.

By the same token, a leader knows when to try something new.

Many salespeople confuse leadership with manipulation. With rare exceptions, manipulators are not particularly good leaders because people have difficulty trusting them. It's tough to inspire people who don't trust you.

A disproportionately high number of top corporate executives were, at an earlier point in their career, highly successful salespeople. Doesn't that tell you that there's something in the nature of what you're doing for a living that helps build bridges, and partnerships, and long-term alliances? Doesn't that tell you that solving the problems of others on a professional level has something important in common with the ultimate leadership role in an organization?

Throughout the sales cycle, you must project the professional image of the leader with your prospect. That doesn't mean you order the prospect around. (God forbid!) It means you take the time to hear the prospect's problems in their entirety—then bring to bear the full weight of what you have to offer in solving those problems. That way, when you finally do say, "Follow me," it won't be overbearing or sound like it's coming out of the blue. It will be the most natural thing in the world, because you have a plan.

But if you make the effort to develop that plan, if you do your homework, and if you incorporate the prospect's concerns every step of the way—you can say, with every right, "Follow me." And the prospect will follow you.

Sales Technique #71

Write the Contract

In any negotiation, there's a big advantage to being the person who writes the final contract. This will give you the upper hand, because when it comes down to it, contracts are words, and the person who writes the final words has the advantage. You can shape the precise terms of the agreement to your liking, and you can make sure nothing slips by you.

I think most people involved in negotiations are honest. But that doesn't stop them from trying to get the best deal possible. After all, that's their job. And it's your job when you're negotiating to pay attention to every last detail of the contract. Because once your signature (or that of your boss) goes on it, you'll have to carry it out.

I was once in negotiations over a compensation package that I had offered to a salesperson I wanted to hire. We went back and forth about it, but in the end, we were able to hammer out a deal. Furthermore, my lawyers wrote the final agreement that everyone signed. That meant it was ten times more favorable than if the salesperson and his representative had drawn up the papers. I don't mean to imply here that I was trying to pull a fast one. My point is simply that the papers set out an agenda. And under all circumstances, it's best if you write the agenda.

It won't do to skim the contracts at the time of signing. In fact, it's best if you can read through them when you're completely free of distractions and can dwell on the meaning of every word and phrase.

Don't rush reading the final contract for a deal. Take your time. When you're looking at the details of a negotiation, especially at the final agreement that's going to come out of it, you have to assume that all the parties involved understand their best interests and are going to act on them. It won't do you any good after a deal is signed to say, "Oh, I didn't really mean that part. Can't we just forget we agreed on that?" If you accidentally agreed to something that's in the interests of your opponent, she or he isn't going to give it back to you.

When you're coming to a final agreement, assume the worst possible scenario. This tactic grows out of what's called the Law of Unintended Consequences. Simply put, this law says that action you take on purpose will produce unexpected results.

In the fifties and sixties, city planners noticed that traffic congestion in big cities was getting worse. More and more people were able to afford cars and were driving them to more places.

The urban planners assumed—pretty reasonably, you'll have to admit—that since people were driving more, they'd need more roads. More roads would mean fewer cars per road and would help relieve the congestion. The result was a great burst of road building. In my home, New York City, urban planner Robert Moses launched a massive series of controversial highway-building projects.

However, when the highways were built, not only did they not relieve congestion, but traffic was worse than ever. Drivers experienced backups that lasted for hours, with all the attendant frustration.

What happened?

The planners failed to foresee that creating more streets would encourage people to purchase and drive more cars. The number of cars on the road expanded to meet the availability of places to drive them. And the traffic problem got worse instead of better.

The point here is that in any agreement you make, there are going to be unintended consequences. Before you sign the deal, sit down and think through all the things that could go wrong if you sign the deal. Not that you shouldn't sign it, but you have to be ready for some of the unintended outcomes it will give rise to.

Some of these you'll be able to anticipate in the contract's language. Some you won't. But the more thought you give to the language of the deal, the better prepared you'll be.

Sales Technique #72

Always Come Back to the Table

It's possible—I've done this myself on more than one occasion—that in the middle of a particularly tough negotiation you've gotten up, stalked to the door, told the other party what you think of them and their organization, and walked out. Emotionally, there's something deeply satisfying about slamming a door. It closes out all the negative energy bubbling and frothing on the other side and puts a barrier between it and you.

If you've done this, chances are you said to yourself, "Well, at least I never have to see *those people* again!"

And then—which has also happened to me—something happened. Maybe your boss decided you had to reopen talks. Maybe the relationship of forces between your two organizations shifted somehow. Whatever the case, you found yourself sitting at a table, the same group of faces staring back at you, and they were all smirking.

Never, you discovered, is a very, very long time.

It's quite possible, of course, that the negotiations to which you're returning ended on a much friendlier note. Sometimes it's possible to walk away from talks with both sides leaving open the possibility of resuming them in the future. Whatever the case, there are some general rules that apply when you're starting over again:

- Don't have preconceptions. The world hasn't stood still since you last spoke to the people sitting on the other side of the table. A lot has happened, both in your organization and theirs. Their objectives have probably shifted, as have yours. So you need to start by determining what's now important to them. And the way to do that? You guessed it. Start asking questions.
- Put the past away. If this negotiation is going to go anywhere, you can't keep letting your mind go back to the time when the guy you're talking to dissed you or made you feel two feet tall. You can't keep looking backward and expect to walk ahead.

- Don't forget the past. This may seem to contradict what I just said, but it really doesn't. You don't need to focus on all the bad moments of your past negotiation. But you shouldn't start with a completely clean slate either, because that would mean you didn't learn anything. If this negotiator's style is to try to push your buttons, remember it. If she has certain hot buttons, remember what they are.

- Be honest, and assume your client is honest until proven otherwise. Whatever may have happened in your previous talks, you should start with the idea that you both want to win and that your goals overlap enough to make a solution possible.

  Especially when your negotiations have broken off on a friendly note, it's to your advantage to make the first move to reopen them.

  - It puts you in control of the negotiation.
  - It demonstrates your desire to make the deal.
  - Psychologically, it makes you appear the stronger of the two parties.

When you first begin your talks again, it's important that you start by taking note of what's changed. Remember, it's not only possible, it's probable that your client's objectives have been altered, so you need to acknowledge this.

A salesperson-client relationship can be like a marriage. There are ups and downs, good times and bad, and sometimes you just get on each other's nerves. In the worst cases, you divorce. Or, in the case of a business relationship, you stalk out of the negotiations and bang the door behind you.

How can you possibly come back to the table after that kind of scene? Believe me, it's not easy. I have as healthy an ego as the next person, and I don't like admitting I was hasty. So it's very wrenching to have to go back to the table when you swore you'd never talk to the other party.

But sometimes, like a marriage, a negotiation that seems dead can be saved. There are just a couple of points to concentrate on:

- Never try to force the other party to say she or he was in the wrong. Every negotiation, whether we admit it to ourselves or not, is a little bit about ego. Nobody likes saying they were mistaken, and there's nothing to be gained from demanding such a confession. Instead, focus on the issues at hand, not what was said at the last session.
- Try to get a consensus on what you agreed on already. Go through the major points of convergence from your previous negotiation and make sure everyone's still okay with them. This will give you a framework for the rest of the discussion.
- Watch out for the words, demands, attitudes, and anything else that derailed the negotiations last time. If you know your opponent is pushing your buttons, push back and let him know you know what he's doing. Above all, avoid a repeat of the behavior that led to the breakdown of the first negotiation.

Ideally, it's great if you can negotiate with different people, but that's not always possible. That's why you've got to, as much as you can, keep the personal out of the discussion. Remember that you don't have to like the client; you just have to do a successful deal with her or him.

Sales Technique #73

Don't Take It Personally

For a salesperson, a rejection is not a personal affront but rather part of the overall cycle inherent in any day's work.

You simply must learn to look at the issue in this way. After all, there's only one sure-fire way to avoid rejection—though it does work like a charm. That way is never to ask for anything. Don't ask for the appointment; don't ask for the sale; don't try to show your prospect how you can help solve problems. You'll never get rejected. Unfortunately, you'll never make any money, either.

One man I worked with, Frank, was trying to make the transition from work as an administrator to a job as a field sales representative. He went into the new position with high hopes. After all, he was a people person. He loved talking about his product. And he knew it inside and out.

However, he was not prepared for the amount of work he had to do to make his efforts worthwhile. He learned in short order that, to get to a realistic number of "yes" answers, he had to be willing to listen to a lot of "no" answers. And that was tough for him.

Frank had worked for fifteen years in a totally different environment. He had grown used to working for weeks on a proposal, having that proposal passed around and returned to him with suggestions, and then putting together another draft—a draft everyone believed in.

Now he was asking himself to move from that slow, consensus-oriented job to a rapid-fire, binary, on-or-off world that profoundly confused him.

He said to me, "Steve, it's not a matter of my not knowing that rejection is part of the cycle. I know how many people I have to see to make money; that's how many people I see. And I'm doing all right. But I'm completely stressed out. I guess it's more a problem of me believing that when people turn down my product, they're really turning me down. And that's hard for me to adjust to at this point. I wish I could change the way I look at things; I know I've tried."

Ultimately, Frank decided that sales wasn't for him; and looking back on it, I'd have to agree with him.

Now, I'm not telling you this story to convince you that if you don't like rejection, you should get out of sales. Nobody likes rejection, and it's natural to feel some disappointment when you hear someone say "no."

But if you can teach yourself to accept that the fact the person says "no" is not a reflection on you, your product, or your company, but merely in the course of things, you can dust yourself off and move on to the next prospect.

Whether you realize it now or not, the main obstacle in approaching the issue of rejection is not how the prospect thinks of you, but how you think of yourself. Don't be too hard on yourself; accept steady progress happily. If you can eventually make the necessary adjustments, and not take rejection personally, you'll be on your way to sales success.

Sales Technique #74

Win Well, Lose Better

"Winning," famed football coach Vince Lombardi said, "isn't every-thing. But the will to win is everything." Every salesperson should keep that quote on a card in her or his pocket and take it out just before walking into a sales call.

You can't win unless you believe in your product or service and unless you believe in yourself.

If you use the techniques outlined in this book, you'll better position yourself to win sales. Not all the time—no one can do that—but most of the time. And it's important that when the chairs are pushed back and everyone stands up and stretches and shakes hands, you know when you've won and when you've lost. It's equally important that you know how to behave under both those circumstances.

Three or four years ago, I was present when a sales rep finished up a negotiation. It had been a very tough slog, and it had taken several days. There were times when it looked as if the whole deal was going to fall apart. In the end, the rep got a deal, but it wasn't nearly what he wanted.

When he and the client put their signatures on the contract, the client stuck out his hand with some innocuous comment about how it had been a good, hard session but he was glad they'd arrived at an agreement.

The rep barely touched the outstretched hand, didn't look the client in the face, let his shoulders slump, and gave an incoherent grunt. Then he slouched out of the room without saying goodbye.

The client just stood staring after him with his mouth open.

Losing a deal is never pleasant, but letting it affect your whole attitude, as the rep did, makes the situation ten times worse. Let's look at what happened.

First, even though the rep didn't get everything he wanted, *he got the sale.* That is, he got something rather than nothing. So he had that much to celebrate, at least.

Second, he made his defeat seem personal, as if somehow it was a comment on him and his abilities. By walking the borderline of rude with his customer, he raised doubts in the client's mind about how serious he could be about holding up his end of the bargain. Behavior such as he exhibited spoke volumes about how well this deal was likely to go.

If someone you just struck a complex deal with behaved like that, would you trust them or the company they represented? Would you want to do business with them again?

I didn't think so.

On some level, selling is about perception. And the last thing you want to be perceived as is a loser. If you look defeated, the next time you sit across the table from your opponent, she'll know how you react to setbacks. And she can use that information to push you further than you want to go.

If it's bad to be a sore loser, it's equally bad to be a vindictive or boastful winner. In truth, the best kind of win for you is if you can align your interests and those of your client so that you both benefit from the deal you're putting together. But there are many points in any negotiation where you definitely want to come out in the best position, often at the expense of the person you're negotiating with. Those range from getting the client to agree to a higher price for your product to convincing him to take a new line of widgets from you.

This means that it's quite possible your opponent will realize that he's lost—he paid more than he intended or wound up getting products he didn't really want. If you try to rub in the fact that you accomplished what you set out to do in the session, chances are that he'll turn sullen or angry, and your relationship will be imperiled.

I keep saying, for you winning ultimately means *getting the sale*. And not just now but in the future. Why risk your client's goodwill for the sake of some cheap crowing because he agreed to pay a price that's higher than the one your last client agreed to?

If you've won, be nice about it. Point out to your opponent the benefits to him or her. Immediately follow up with practical suggestions for implementation, so the other party knows how enthusiastic you are about this deal.

Once again, body language is important. Firm, purposeful movements convey a sense of confidence and control. Always look your client full in the face when you're speaking to her, and never allow yourself to do anything or say anything that could be interpreted as gloating. (One rep I know, after closing a deal, remarked to his client, "Man, I was afraid you were going to hold out for a much lower price." The client looked at him for a moment then said, "Next time I will." And he did.)

Winning is about substance, of course. But it's also important that you frame your win in such a way that your boss and your company and the company's shareholders understand what you won. As much as possible, you should also try to help your client achieve the same thing. When both sides understand what they've won, they'll be best able to act upon it.

The most likely scenario in any negotiation is that neither party will entirely win or lose. You'll give on some points and get on others. Sometimes the talks may take a turn that neither of you anticipated, and you'll find a solution that makes both of you happy. Calvin (of *Calvin and Hobbes*) once remarked with the cynicism of a six-year-old, "A good compromise leaves everybody mad." Actually, in my experience a good compromise is one that leaves both parties thinking they got what they needed. It may well be that by conceding on nonessential points, you'll win the big issue that's important to you.

Sales Technique #75

Look Beyond the Close

The other day I was driving on the Long Island Expressway, and I was able to avert an accident because I was looking, not at the car in front of me, but at the car two cars in front of me. I saw his lights go on first, and I stopped in time to avoid slamming into someone.

That's the kind of thinking that's necessary for long-term success in sales. One of the big differences between successful salespeople and salespeople who don't succeed is that successful salespeople are better able to anticipate what's going to happen in the industries they sell to. They understand what's going on in the worlds that affect the worlds their customers live and work in

You can anticipate and prepare for the obstacles your prospects and customers face. You can read the journals and industry publications that affect key industries in your prospect and customer base. You can develop networks that keep you fully informed. That means you can anticipate the responses you're likely to get. Successful salespeople learn to anticipate the objections or responses of their prospects, and they learn to prepare themselves and their organizations. They ask themselves, "What can I anticipate? What trends are emerging in industries that affect this industry? What's going to happen two car lengths ahead of me?"

When was the last time you revised your sales materials, based on new information you received from an industry trade magazine, a discussion with a key contact, or an update from the Internet? Sure, your company gives you materials, but there's no law preventing you from setting up revised versions, updating copy, or changing the questions you ask or the order in which you ask them.

The successful salesperson stays informed and constantly updates his or her anticipated sales dialogues and materials as a result of what he's learned. The successful salesperson *doesn't* wait for change to happen, but rather anticipates change and makes a habit of looking two cars ahead.

CONCLUSION

Fifteen years ago, surveying the sales landscape, I would have said that it all looked pretty familiar. There were some things such as e-mail that were beginning to make an impact, but overall nothing much had changed from when I started in this business.

Today, I can't say that. The field of sales—and of business—is changing every year (sometimes every month). And there's no indication that it's going to stabilize any time soon.

Change, in other words, is the new normal. The faster you accept that, the better a salesperson you're going to be.

The Great Recession came as a huge shock to many people precisely because it was so unanticipated. Many people, looking at the state of the economy in 2006 and 2007, assumed that housing prices would continue to go up, that the economy would expand forever, and that the bankers and brokers dealing in strangely named things like "derivatives" and "credit swaps" actually knew what they were doing. None of that, of course, was the case. And a lot of salespeople were so taken aback by events that they felt as if selling were no longer possible.

I didn't believe that. In fact, I wrote a book, *Selling When No One Is Buying*, precisely to refute that idea. The theme of that book was simple: even though the landscape has changed, the fundamentals of selling haven't.

187

You still have to ask questions.

You still have to put the client front and center.

You still have to have confidence in yourself and what you're selling.

The status quo is your competition, but that doesn't mean you can ignore the basics of selling. It just means you have to adapt them to different circumstances. That's been the theme running through this book.

So take these techniques, master them, and go out and sell!

Stephan Schiffman
New York City
May 2012

APPENDIX A

SAMPLE COLD CALLING SCRIPTS

Almost every product that you buy today has a set of instructions; many even state something along the lines of "use only as directed." I take a slightly different approach on the matter of tinkering with the simple prospecting scripts that follow. Certainly you should feel free to adapt them to your own personal style. But do so in keeping with the spirit of the program outlined in this book. Don't overembellish.

As you look these scripts over, you may find them a little ambitious. They're meant to be. They're simple, and they're direct. That's why they work.

At one of my seminars, a group of salespeople expressed some reservations about these scripts. Why were they so aggressive? Where were the probing questions? How were they to "draw the prospects in"?

Their problem, of course, was that they were wasting their time talking to people they should have classified as simple rejections in the first minute of the conversation. And anyway, selling over the phone is not what cold calling is about.

To address the concerns these people raised, I decided to try a little experiment. I sat down one Tuesday and made seven cold calls in a two-hour period. I got through to two people and got one appointment by using one of the scripts reproduced here—word for word.

That's 50 percent. I asked the sales manager if he could match that figure using his current methods. He couldn't.

When the salespeople finally saw the results of the program, they decided to give it a try.

The salespeople I'm talking about were lucky. They kept an open mind. If you do the same thing, you'll see a marked improvement in your performance.

The scripts outlined here are the basis for the work you're about to undertake. Obviously, as you get more proficient at your phone prospecting work, you'll change a word here and there to fit your own style and requirements. But the same approach applies—and that's the point. You'll stop wasting time by having extended conversations on the phone. You'll be direct in asking for the appointment. You'll know what you're going to say in advance.

When I start my seminars, I usually begin with the sentence, "When God wanted to punish salespeople, he invented the cold call." That actually sums up my feelings, and possibly yours as well, about the cold call. You, and only you, can turn that "curse" into an opportunity—by beginning to use the techniques I've shown you, and the scripts provided here.

INITIAL CONTACT SCRIPT

Good morning _____ , this is _____ from _____ .
    The reason I'm calling you today specifically is so I can stop by and tell you about our new _____ program that increases _____ . I'm sure that you, like _____ , are interested in _____ .

(Positive response).

That's great _____ ; let's get together. How's _____ ?

THIRD-PARTY ENDORSEMENT SCRIPT

Good morning _____ , this is _____ from _____ . *(Insert your brief commercial on your company.)* The reason I'm calling you today specifically is that we've just completed working on a major project for _____ , which was extremely successful in increasing _____ . What I'd like to do is stop by next _____ to tell you about the success I had at _____ . How's _____ ?

REFERRAL SCRIPT

Good morning _____ , this is _____ . *(Insert your brief commercial on your company.)* The reason I'm calling you today specifically is that _____ just suggested I give you a call to set up an appointment. I wanted to know if _____ at _____ would be okay.

FOLLOW-UP SCRIPT

Good morning _____ , this is _____ from _____ . A number of weeks ago I contacted you, and you asked me to call you back today to set up an appointment. Would _____ be good for you?

APPENDIX B

NINE KEY PRINCIPLES
OF SALES SUCCESS

My only real concern when it comes to sales training is whether the training I offer helps people make more sales. If it doesn't, then the training really doesn't make any difference. The purpose of sales training is to help people do what they do—that is, sell—better—that is, make more sales.

With that aim in mind, let's look now at some of the basic principles for sales success. If you only memorize one portion of this book, make it this one!

1. All Steps Lead to the Next Step

The only reason you're making a cold call is to get an appointment. The only reason you went on the appointment is to get to the next step in your sale. Your next step could be the second appointment or it could be a close. It doesn't really matter to me what it is, as long as you know what it is. Too many salespeople go on appointments without having any idea what their objective for the visit is.

The objective of every step of the sales process is to get to the next step. If what you're doing doesn't get you to the next step, do something else that does!

2. The Difference Between Success and Failure Is Seventy-Two Hours

I think each and every one of us has had a great idea that went unattended. We said, "Boy, I ought to write a book about that," or, "That's a great idea for a movie," or, "I should design something that does that better." Then, six months or a year later we see that our idea has actually been implemented by someone else. Well, what happened? The difference was that the other person took action on the idea.

You can read this book, but if you don't begin to implement the concepts that we've talked about here within seventy-two hours, and then maintain the activity for twenty-one days, you're not going to be successful.

People tend to fall back on what they know. And if you don't get started with these concepts within seventy-two hours, you'll fall back on what you already know, and you'll have missed an opportunity to be far more successful than you are now. Respond immediately! Find something to implement! Take action now!

Changing your selling techniques within seventy-two hours really is the key to success.

3. All Objections and Responses Can and Should Be Anticipated

Everything that I've ever created in selling has been based on the premise that I can know in advance what a prospect's response will be—that I can learn to predict how people will respond to me during a cold call or in person.

I know, for example, that on a sales call I'm going to be asked certain questions about my training techniques and about how my seminars work. I'm prepared for these questions. I have my answers ready. If I didn't prepare an answer, that would be like going on a sales call without a business card. I would never do that. Would you?

4. Follow-Through Is an Integral Part of Sales

I prefer "follow-through" to "follow-up." Don't you? In fact, I very rarely say to anybody, "I'm going to follow up with a telephone call." What I like to say is "I'm going to follow through by calling you next week." In other words, I'm going to follow through on what I've started. I'm going to complete it. I may not make every sale, but I'm going to follow each relationship through as far as I can.

5. You Must Find Out What the Prospect Does

Find out what people do! Ask them what they do, how they do it, when they do it, where they do it, who they do it with, and why they do it that way. Your job is to help them do it better.

6. Prospects Respond in Kind

I've said it throughout this book, and I'll say it again here. People respond to what you're asking, and they respond in kind to how you ask. As I've pointed out repeatedly, if you ask, "Do you need my service?" the odds are you're going to hear a "no." If you talk instead about how you can help them do what they do better, you're going to be successful.

This concept of asking the right questions comes from a discussion Socrates and Plato had about pleasing the gods. They concluded that the pious person was the person who pleased the gods; that is, who made the gods happy. I believe that, in order to make the gods happy, we have to ask the question, "What, exactly, will make them happy?" Therefore, to my way of thinking, a pious person is one who asks the key questions.

If you don't ask questions like "What is it that you do?" or "What are you trying to get accomplished?" you will not get the success you deserve.

7. It's Necessary to Ask for the Appointment

One of the biggest mistakes salespeople make is failing to ask for the appointment. I've heard salespeople ask for just about everything except an appointment during a cold call. Guess what? They don't get the appointment!

8. It's Necessary to Understand the Four P's

In order to become a more successful salesperson, you should concern yourself with four basic areas of knowledge:

- Professional development
- Product malleability
- Presentation skills
- Prospecting

Let's look at each of them in turn:

Professional Development

Ninety percent of all salespeople in the United States fail to read one book about improving their sales techniques in a given year. Furthermore, most salespeople will not pay for their own sales training; 90 percent of all sales training is paid for by the employer. Salespeople will pay for their own swimming lessons, quilting lessons, riding lessons, tennis lessons, horseback riding lessons, driving lessons, and (of course) golf lessons, but they won't pay for their own sales training. You may want to give some thought to whether or not you need to sign up for a program that will help you improve your sales skills. (You've already beaten the odds, however, by reading a sales-related book!)

Product Malleability

"Product malleability" means repositioning your product or service to fit your prospect's specific needs.

Remember, the purpose of your product is to help people do what they do better. Strictly speaking, your product doesn't matter as much as your ability to take it and apply it—and that means, of course, that you have to understand your prospect's business. So product malleability comes from your understanding of what your prospect does, and how you can apply what you offer to the prospect's unique situation.

Presentation Skills

Presentation skills account for an important part of your overall success, but they probably aren't as important as you might think at first. Many people practice their presentations constantly, using role-playing, memorization, and even video-taping to hone their "moment" with the prospect. Do they realize that the ratio of calls to appointments is usually three-to-one—and sometimes even higher?

I would be foolish if I told you that making a good presentation to your prospect is not important. But in the overall scheme of things, it is still not as important as getting in the door—prospecting. And, of course, no amount of practice can perfect a presentation that is not based on solid information about the prospect.

Prospecting

Prospecting is really what sales success is all about. It's what makes the difference. We did a study of successful salespeople making between $75,000 and $125,000 a year consistently for ten consecutive years. We learned that 45 percent of the success of an individual salesperson comes directly from his or her ability to prospect. Twenty percent comes from presentation skills. Twenty percent comes from product knowledge or product malleability, and the remaining 15 percent comes from sales training. In other words, 65 percent of what successful salespeople do is finding people and talking about potential applications; that's prospecting and presenting combined.

9. It's Necessary to Understand the Three Most Important Words in Sales

The three most important words in sales today are *obsession, utilization,* and *implementation.* Let's consider those:

Obsession

You need to be obsessed by what you're doing. You have to be willing to think about your job seven days a week, twenty-four hours a day.

Utilization

Obsession without discipline results in chaos. If you're not disciplined enough to stay focused, to make the calls, to do what you have to do to reach your goals, you're not going to be successful. Successful people understand how to utilize everything. So take all the material, all the things that you've read in this book, and use as much as you possibly can to become more successful.

Implementation

And finally, we come to implementation. You just have to do it. You have to implement the plan. You have to do the work. If you don't do it, you're not going to be successful.

APPENDIX C

TEN TRAITS OF SUCCESSFUL SALESPEOPLE

In all the years that I've traveled and during all the programs I've done, I've given more than 8,000 speeches and trained more than a half million salespeople. I've found that there are certain key characteristics that make people successful in sales. Here are the top ten.

1. They're Not Normal

You've decided to go into sales and, therefore, by the very definition, you're not normal. Sales success is not a normal state. Sales success is not normal—because success means being willing to act differently. When you're successful, you're not normal, and because you're going to maintain that success, you're comfortable with the idea of never being normal again!

2. They're Committed

Successful salespeople are committed to their goals, and they have goals. Not only do you have to be committed to your own goals, but you have to be committed to the goals of your company. Do you understand those goals? Do you understand fully what your company is trying to accomplish?

You're also looking to work with the goals of your customers. As soon as salespeople say to me that they're concerned about their commission checks, then I start worrying whether or not they're concerned about their customers. If you help customers accomplish their goals, if you help them do what they do better, you will never, ever lose.

3. They're Motivated

Successful salespeople are self-motivated. They know what they have to do and they know how they're going to get there. Interestingly enough, the role of the sales manager in the successful salesperson's career is really minimal. You and I both know what we have to do. We know we have to make calls. We know we have to follow through and do the things you've been reading about in this book each and every day. We know we have to take action. We have to make things happen.

One of my favorite stories is about a great Hollywood literary agent named Swifty Lazar. His actual name was Irving, but everybody in the business called him Swifty. Swifty Lazar died a number of years ago, but in reading about him, one of the things that struck me was that every single morning, he said he would get up and he would look at his calendar and see what was going to happen that day. And if there was nothing that was going to happen, he made something happen every day . . . before lunch! And that's exactly my philosophy—you make something happen every day . . . before lunch. You get an appointment. You make a call. You start some activity. Because the activity you create today is going to give you business down the road.

4. They're Self-Declared

Being self-declared means that successful salespeople feel good about themselves. Successful salespeople carry themselves well, they talk themselves up, and they understand what it is they have to accomplish and how they're going to get there.

5. They Sacrifice

If you've ever watched the Olympics, or any committed athlete, you realize that an athlete makes tremendous sacrifices. They make choices each and every day in order to be successful. They understand that the gain is worth the choice that they're going to make.

6. They Delegate

Successful salespeople also understand how to prioritize and how to get the things they need to do done. They know how to take best advantage of the resources and the people available to them.

7. They're Optimistic

Successful salespeople are part of the solution and not part of the problem. It's easy to find problems. Anyone can do that. And yet I'll bet the person you remember most in life, the person you consider your mentor (whether it's your parent, grandparent, coach, or a college professor), is the person who helped you find the solutions.

Successful people are believers. They believe the great mission can be accomplished. They not only believe it; they live it.

8. They're Enthusiastic

I absolutely, positively love doing what I do. The reason I tell you that is that I want you to be enthusiastic each and every day. Every single day, get up as if it were the first day you've ever sold. Do you remember the very first sales call you went on? Remember that anxiety, that nervousness, the adrenaline pumping through your body? It was exciting! Live that excitement every day!

9. They Live Off-Peak

Successful salespeople don't drive onto the highway at 8:30 A.M. and sit in traffic. They're going earlier, or they're going later. They're not going with everybody else.

They constantly rethink their options. They're not standing in line at noon for a restaurant. They go earlier or later. They're not like the woman in New York City I heard of recently who stood in line for an hour and a half . . . to complain about the lines.

10. They're Consistent and Persistent

Successful salespeople have the focus and the discipline to follow through on their projects and not get bored. Successful salespeople aren't fickle. They have a plan and stick with it.

Appendix D

Seven Questions You Should Be Able to Answer Before You Try to Close the Deal

Why do salespeople fall into the trap of attempting to close the sale with silly "closing tricks"—like saying "I'll lose my job if you don't buy from me?" The short answer is that they're afraid. Specifically, they're afraid the prospect will turn them down if they ask for the business straightforwardly. So to overcome this fear, they practice delivering some manipulative, supposedly foolproof "technique" that somehow will magically make the person say "Yes."

The truth is, their fear about asking for the business is usually well justified. Most salespeople who try to close the deal don't yet know enough about the other person to ask for the business.

Here are seven questions you should be sure to ask your prospect before you attempt to close any sale. If you don't know the answers . . . you're not yet ready to make a formal recommendation. You should get face-to-face with your prospect, pull out your pen and your yellow legal pad, and find out the answers.

And by the way—asking these questions also serves an important purpose during the course of your discussion with the prospect. By posing a question that addresses one of the following issues and then taking notes on the response you receive, you regain control of the conversation and put yourself in a better position to make a recommendation about the next step in the relationship.

1. How did this person get this job?

Was your contact one of the founders of the company? Was he or she recruited by a pricey executive search firm? Did he or she answer a classified ad a month and a half ago? Your aim here is to determine your contact's level of influence.

2. What's the person's role in the organization?

Is your contact a leader or a follower? What part did he or she play in the past when it came to deciding whether and how to use companies like yours? What major projects is he or she working on right now? If the person you're talking to does not have any projects that are relevant to your selling area, you are not talking to the right person. Your aim here is to find out what this person can or cannot do within the organization.

3. Are you dealing with someone who is either (a) a decision maker or (b) a person who can get the decision made for you?

If your contact has no knowledge, access, or influence relating to your product or service, you need to find a way to get this person to help you connect with someone else in the organization. Your aim here is to identify who, in the organization, is likely to be able to help you get this deal done—and to determine with some certainty whether your contact falls into that category.

4. What's the organization's current plan for dealing with the area where you hope to make a contribution?

To find out, ask, "What were you planning to do this quarter in order to . . . ?" Your aim here is to identify any competitors who may already be involved, and to get a sense of how the target organization has defined the problem up to this point.

5. Why aren't they using you already?

Your aim here is twofold: to learn what the company already knows or thinks about your organization, and to find out what plans are already in place. (To this extent, there is a certain amount of overlap between this question and #4.) I suggest that, early on in the relationship, you ask some variation on this question: "I checked my records and I noticed you're not using us right now. I'm just curious—why not?" While you're at it, you could also find out if the company ever considered working with you or getting in touch with you in the past. You may have been on the short-list for a project and not even known about it.

6. Does this deal truly make sense to the other person?

The goal here is to find out whether you're on your own or whether you've got an ally. Sometimes salespeople ask, "How am I supposed to know whether or not what I'm proposing makes sense to the other person?" The answer is actually very simple. When the prospect begins to act as though closing the sale is as important to him or her as it is to you . . . you'll know it makes sense! I like to find out whether what I'm discussing with a prospect really makes sense by asking a question like this as I'm on the way out the door after a second meeting: "Listen— just between you and me, how do you think this is going to turn out?"

7. What does your contact think is going to happen next?

The idea here is to get clear on what the mutually agreed-upon next step in the relationship is. If your contact has no idea you're about to close the deal, there's a problem. Here's a good selling rule: Never make a presentation you don't think will close! Try saying something like: "You know, based on what we've gone over today, I have to say that this really makes sense to me. I'm thinking that the next time we get together, on Tuesday at 2:00, we'll go over all the changes and I'll show you our full proposal, and at that point, I think it's going to make sense for us to reserve the training dates. What do you think?"

APPENDIX E

THE FIVE STAGES
OF THE SALES CAREER

There are five distinct stages to the sales career, five periods of professional change growth that apply specifically to the sales professional. If
you manage people who sell for a living, you should know what these
five stages are!

1. The Novice

The Novice relies heavily on other team members; he or she is still
in the "learning the ropes" phase. The Novice may place too much
importance on a single prospect and neglect the importance of effective prospect management.

2. The Contributor

The Contributor works more autonomously than the Novice, and
can anticipate prospect expectations and manage the sales cycle more
effectively. Contributors tend to be strongly goal oriented and to show
a great deal of commitment to their work. They need less help than
Novices when it comes to managing their own time, gathering the

unique prospect information necessary to develop the right "proposal," and closing the sale. A common challenge is an unwillingness to reach out to other team members for help in securing larger and more complex deals.

3. The Performer

The Performer serves as a role model for others in the sales organization and assists in the completion of large and complex sales. Performers tend to have a deep experience base and superior people skills. They support and motivate other team members in support of their key goals. These are usually the supreme "team players." Some (but by no means all) Performers may become impatient with less experienced colleagues.

4. The Leader

The Leader chooses to assume a coordinating role in the sales team's activities; he or she is also comfortable developing and supporting new talent. Leaders can articulate the company vision and support key partnerships that arise within the sales team. Effective Leaders know how to win group support for new and challenging goals established by the higher-ups in the organization. Many Leaders find that balancing work and personal spheres can be a challenge.

5. The Builder

The Builder channels his or her entire personality into the mission of building the company, often at the expense of family ties. Builders are so committed to the long-term success of the group that they are often compared to people with religious callings or vocations. It really is a matter of faith to them that the company should overcome competitive and market challenges, grow, and prosper in the long term. Most chief executives and presidents are still very much salespeople regardless of their title. Whatever their job title, these salespeople tend to have superior executive, team building, and long-term strategic abilities. Their own high standards and extraordinary commitment are other important assets. A common challenge area for the Builder is that others may perceive him or her as eccentric, paradoxical or even autocratic.

■ ■ ■

Those are the five stages. You need not move all the way forward to the Builder stage to experience a satisfying career, but you should be able to identify where you are . . . and where you want to be . . . within this model. Trying to perform at one level before one has mastered the responsibilities of the previous level leads to what I call "stage uncertainty." This kind of uncertainty—on the part of the manager or the salesperson—is a major contributor to unhealthy stress and early burnout.

Finally, note this well: A salesperson's years of experience on the job may have nothing whatsoever to do with the stage he or she occupies. Seniority in sales is not the same as ability!

INDEX

About the Author

Stephan Schiffman has trained more than 500,000 salespeople at firms such as AT&T Information Systems, Chemical Bank, Manufacturer's Hanover Trust, Motorola, and U.S. Health Care. He is the author of such bestselling books as *Cold Calling Techniques (That Really Work!)* and *Closing Techniques (That Really Work!)*. When not speaking to audiences around the globe about sales and sales training, he lives in New York City.